The Wall of Death

Todd and Soutter Families

1929–1960s

The Wall of Death

Todd and Soutter Families

1929–1960s

Ann Wright

JANUS PUBLISHING COMPANY LTD
Cambridge, England

First published in Great Britain 2018
by Janus Publishing Company Ltd
The Studio
High Green
Great Shelford
Cambridge CB22 5EG

www.januspublishing.co.uk

British Library Cataloguing-in-Publication Data
A catalogue record for this book is available from the British Library

ISBN 978-1-85756-873-8

Cover Design: Janus Publishing
Cover Image: Supplied by the Author

Printed and bound in Great Britain

Contents

The Todd and Soutter Families

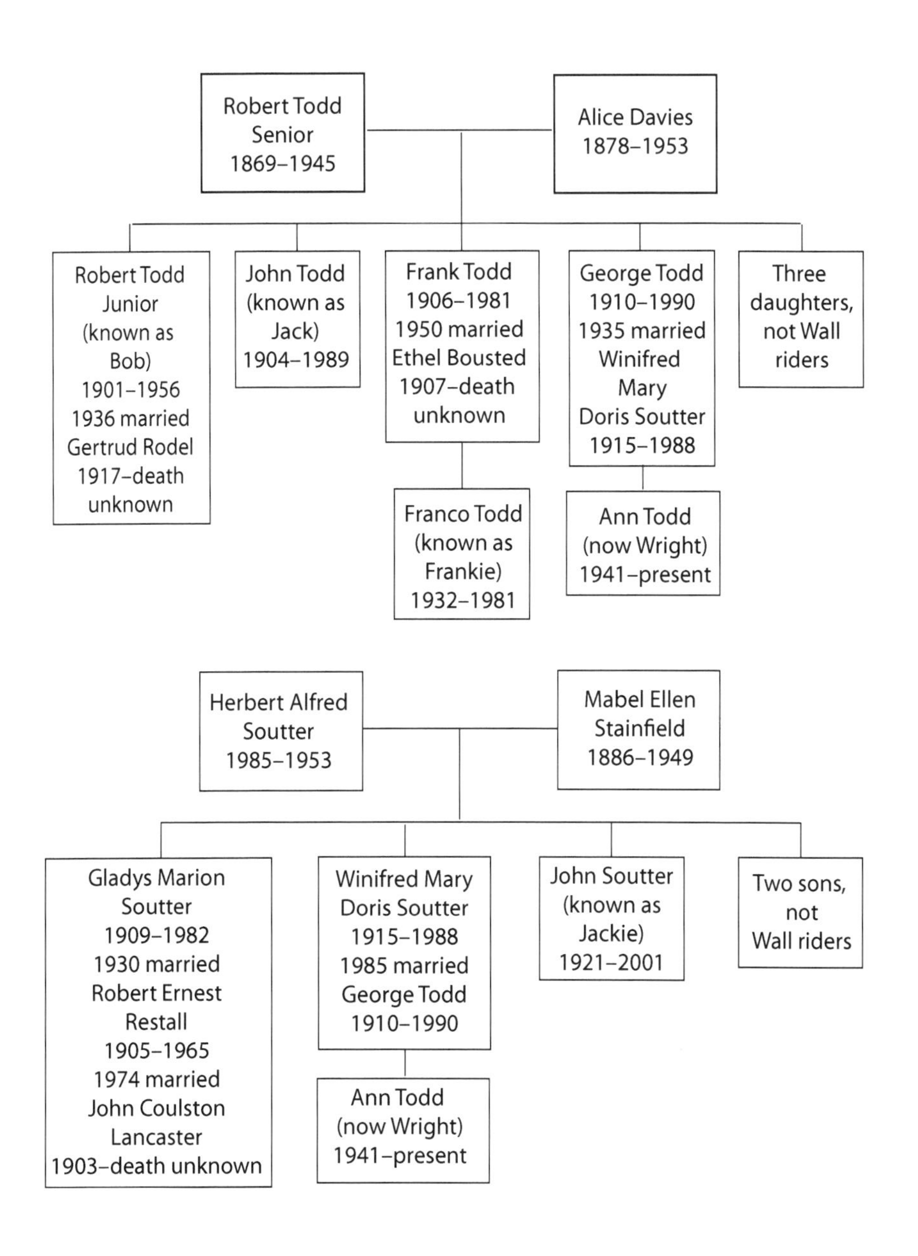

Foreword

I was born in 1941 in a caravan, parked in a field, on a farm in Banwell, Somerset. My family were not farmers. My mother, Winifred Todd, was in labour for two days. After the birth the doctor advised her not to have any more children. The reason was that my mother was and had been for eleven years a Wall of Death rider and, apparently, her very strong muscles made the birth so very difficult, not helped, I imagine, by the fact that the birth was in a caravan and not a hospital.

What I did not know was that I had been born into an extraordinary family of Wall of Death riders. By 1941 my mother was an owner/rider, my aunt was an owner/rider and married to a rider, and one of their brothers was a rider. My father was a Wall of Death owner/rider, his three brothers were also owner/riders, and what is more they were all married to Wall of Death riders. There were, therefore, in 1941, ten riders in my family and later on two more family members were to join them. This is the story of my family. It is not a history of the Wall of Death – for that see Allan Ford and Nick Corble's book *Riding the Wall of Death.* My late parents were wonderful – they enjoyed life, worked extremely hard, played hard, and were very good to their staff, either riders or helpers on the wall. Most people who knew them, even when they were in their seventies, also thought they were an unusual, party-giving, generous couple with amazing stories to tell. This book is dedicated to my late parents, all my other Wall of Death family and to my husband, Ian, our two sons, George and David, and our grandchildren.

I have to acknowledge the help of Ian Wright, my husband, who not only has a phenomenal memory of conversations with my parents and my aunts and uncles but also for the last three years has been bombarded with questions by me about his memories, conversations with relatives and views on what happened when, to whom and why. Thanks also to my sons George and David who advised on the technicalities of my laptop. I also acknowledge the help of Stuart Soutter, my cousin; his mother,

Lesley Soutter, my aunt by marriage; Allan Ford, my Wall of Death friend for many years (www.thewallofdeath.com); Alan Mercer, Wall of Death friend, researcher (see website www.vintagewallofdeath.co.uk); Professor Jonathan Woodham and Dr Paddy Maguire of the University of Brighton who taught me to research when I was an undergraduate; Judith Hayward for the German translations; and Janet Shaw who read the first early draft.

Ann Wright
Email: wod@lawreny.net

Introduction

Popular Culture after WW1 and the Wall of Death

By 1929 there was a huge choice of popular culture available for the British to experience. The public were also experiencing higher real wages, shorter working hours and slightly longer holidays. Day trips and coach outings were popular and by 1931 a million families owned a motor car, rising to 2 million by 1939 and by 1931, 600,000 people owned a motorbike and motor cycling became a popular leisure pursuit with clubs set up all over the UK. Cycling was becoming more common.

Visiting the cinema was the most popular choice of pastime, although mostly by working-class women. Almost every town had a cinema and the managers promoted the films with flyers, hand-outs and newspaper publicity. The theatre was also a draw with a choice of thrillers, detective stories, musical comedy and revue shows. Ivor Novello and Noel Coward were popular and budget musicals were staged in London. Outside London repertory theatre was common and newspapers advertised these a great deal and included reviews. The top ten films were *Gone with the Wind, Snow White and the Seven Dwarfs, The Wizard of Oz, Frankenstein, Ingagi, Top Hat, 42nd Street, Conquest, Damaged Lives* and *Parnell.*

Libraries were opening and reading became commonplace. *The Hobbit, Gone with the Wind, Brave New World, Of Mice and Men, The Grapes of Wrath, Rebecca, And Then There Were None, Murder on the Orient Express* and *The Good Earth* were the top books. For younger people comics were available such as *Flash Gordon* started in 1934. By the end of the 1930s it was published in 130 newspapers, translated into eight languages and read by 50 million people. *Superman, The Phantom* and *Detective Comics* were also published. The wireless also became more common with three-quarters of families holding wireless licences by 1939.

Sport, both spectator and participation, was another choice, especially horse racing, greyhound racing, football, grass-track riding, tennis and rugby.

Dancing and dance bands were very popular with bands like those of Jack Hylton, Duke Ellington and Glen Miller and singers like Judy Garland, Bing Crosby and Frank Sinatra being frequently listened to or seen. Along with this, dancing was enjoyed at various Palais de Dance and there were even dance marathons, like the Jitterbug.

So the Wall of Death had a lot of competition in getting the public to spend their money.

Fairgrounds and amusements parks were frequented, sometimes with thousands of visitors, but perhaps it was the thrill of the Wall of Death which made it so popular.

A Wall of Death is heard and smelt before being seen on an amusement park or fairground. The noise is the roar of motorcycles speeding round a wooden dome, the dome vibrating as the bikes go round, and the back-firing of the engines. There is also the crowd watching inside roaring with gasps of amazement and clapping at the end of each act.

Getting closer, the spieler on the front of the wall is shouting through a microphone to entice the punters in, using such phrases as 'this has to be seen to be believed', 'see dare-devil riders risking their lives on the wall, performing amazing tricks on their motorcycles', 'witness them racing each other round the wall and see them doing the Death Ride'.

Closer up, the crowds are looking on in disbelief watching a rider on a bike which is set up on rollers outside the wall but on the front bally of the wall. The bally is the platform at the front of the wall on which the riders and the spieler stand before a performance inside.

As the rollers go round the bike wheels go round and on the bike is one of the dare-devil riders, usually dressed in an attractive bright outfit. The rider performs a series of amazing tricks, like riding the bike standing up, sitting side-saddle, and sitting with his/her legs over the handlebars. The spieler invites the watching audience to pay to go inside and see these tricks being performed on the vertical wall.

The customers having paid to enter and climbed the steps to the top, the show begins. Here the real thrill is seen and heard – the noise of the bikes, the gasps of astonishment from the watching audience witnessing the death-defying tricks the riders perform on the circling bikes, the audience fearing that the riders might crash because it all looks so dangerous, fearing they might ride over the safety cable at the top into the audience who are amazed at what they see. Two, often three riders ride round at the same time, overtaking each other. All of the riders perform a variety of tricks. You might think there is some magic that keeps them on a vertical wall, perhaps the use of magnets or some other trickery – but there is no trick, it is all down to the unbelievable skill and bravery of the riders and centrifugal force.

In 1929 and the 1930s you would also have seen men and women driving cars on the wall, or a car with a side platform with a live lion sitting on it being driven round – even one with a tiger, a bear or a monkey on the side platform, even a monkey driving its own little car. Or a special act where a man on roller skates was towed round the wall by another rider on a bike. The women were usually in their teens and you would have been amazed at how these young girls appeared to be risking their lives.

That is the thrill of seeing a live Wall of Death – watching it on YouTube is not at all the same experience. There are five walls now operating in the UK – Ken Fox has two, the Messhams have two and a Globe of Death, and Demon Drome have one. They can also be seen on the Continent and always at the Munich Oktoberfest. There are several touring in the USA. The New York Wall of Death Museum has three and there is a new museum in Sweden. You can also see walls on YouTube.

Chapter 1

Riding and Owning a Wall of Death – 1929–1930s

The Wall of Death is a vertical circular cylindrical wooden structure which can vary in height and diameter, but the average is 28–30 feet in diameter and 15–20 feet high. From the circular wooden floor is a wooden sloping banking track which leads the bike from the floor up onto the vertical wall. There is a door in the wall which opens onto the front of the wall – this is how the riders get in and out, their motorcycles being inside, with the exception of the bikes used on the bally. The wall is built up and dismantled by putting up or taking down the eighteen extremely heavy high wooden panels on a circular flat wooden base. Once dismantled the

Author and husband outside Allan Ford's wall 1990s

whole structure is put on a large lorry for transport to another venue. Usually, but not always, the structure has a canopy called a tilt to keep out the rain. The tilt is supported by a high wooden pole, the base of which is set in the centre of the floor. The riders park their bikes around this centre pole and it is where their microphone/megaphone is kept.

Allan Ford's wall – interior 1990s

At the public entrance to the wall there is a wooden pay box to buy tickets and the tickets are collected by a member of staff at the top of the steps. There are two sets of steps on the outside from ground level to the top of the wall for the public to mount and dismount. Once up they stand on the walkround, looking into the wall itself. There is a metal safety cable going round inside the top of the wall to stop the riders from riding out of the top of the vertical wall and onto the walkround and the audience. This has not been completely foolproof; occasionally riders did ride over the safety cable into the watching crowd.

The wall was ridden by men and women on motorcycles and in some instances in cars, and nowadays go-karts and bicycles. Most riders did not wear crash helmets although some did. It was said to be impossible to wear them because of the centrifugal force.

Late in 1930 a reporter gave an idea of what an apprentice rider would go through in learning to ride.[1] However, it was rather inaccurate, saying that it took four months to learn to ride round on the floor and a further few months to learn to ride the wall properly. That was hugely exaggerated and my mother learned to ride in two weeks.

Centrifugal force diagram

The front of the wall, which is what the audience saw from outside, was called the bally. On the bally, trying to attract the crowd to pay to see the show, was the spieler or barker, who announced to the crowds what the audience would see if they entered the show. The language used was rather like this: 'Come and see the dare-devil riders, riding their powerful motorbikes on a perpendicular wall and performing hair-raising and dangerous stunt tricks, which have to be seen to be believed.' The spieler played a crucial role in enticing the public into the show.

There was also a set of rollers outside on the bally, on which one of the riders sat on a motorbike and performed tricks. Sometimes the bally had a roof and the rollers were set on this roof. This was higher up and therefore the demonstration could be seen by more of the crowd watching from the front.

They were not always called Wall of Death; other names were Dome of Death, Drome of Death, Death Wall, Motordrome, The New Motordrome, Autodrome of Death, Demon Drome Wall of Death, Death Riders, Drome of Thrills, Death Circus, The Drome of Satan, Original Dome of Thrills, Cylinder of Death and Silodrome. The latter was an American term so called because walls resembled grain silos. They are not to be confused with the Globe of Death, which was also seen in the twenties and thirties and nowadays occasionally. The globe is a completely circular see-through metal construction, with gates at the bottom through which the riders on motorcycles entered, and which were then closed. It is hoisted above the ground and the audience views it from below. There was one of these apparently at the 1924 British Wembley Exhibition in London. Some riders could ride both the wall and the globe but riders preferred the wall, which they considered to be less dangerous. In the early days it was quite common for there to be a Globe and a Wall of Death at the same fair. For a full and detailed history of how the Wall of Death developed in America before appearing in the UK see Allan Ford and Nick Corble's book.[2]

Riders wore what looked like horse-riding breeches, boots and jackets, often with their riding names in fabric attached to the jackets. They often used glamorous and exciting names when riding and in adverts to attract the public. These names were also painted up on the back of the bally and usually painted on their bikes. This makes research somewhat difficult – quite often the riding names bore no relation to their real names. What is more, some riders used different riding names at different times; for instance, Robert Ernest Restall, the Canadian, used Speedy Bob Lee, Speedy Bob Lew, Speedy Bob, or Bob Lee at various times.

The Showmen's Guild of Great Britain was formerly The United Kingdom Van Dwellers Protection Association, formed in 1888. It became the 'Showmen's and Van Dwellers Protection Association' in 1896 and in 1917 it became a trade union, representing its travelling funfair members. Its purpose was to protect its members by a set of rules, to oversee the proper and safe running of fairs and to challenge Parliament if any laws were to the detriment of its members.

For instance in 1929 new rules were brought in including:

> To promote the interests of the Guild and of its members, lessees of ground who are members of the Guild shall not let ground to persons who are not also members. Likewise no members shall take nor occupy ground from any lessee who is not also a member of the Guild and any person applying for or letting ground shall be required to produce his card of membership, when called up so to do to show that he is a member of the Guild.[3]

Between 1929 and at least 1939 access to sites on fairgrounds was, therefore, strictly organized by the guild. To be a member you had to have been born in a caravan. The important guild showmen, who owned the rights to fairgrounds, were called Riding Masters (relating to the fact that they mostly owned fairground rides, such as gallopers). So Wall of Death owners who were not guild members had to get permission from a Riding Master to appear at a certain fair and the wall usually went under the name of the Riding Master even though it might not be owned by him. The Riding Master would take 40 per cent of the takings, the owner 60 per cent, although these percentages varied.

Walls were transported on heavy-duty lorries, which in the early 1930s were steam driven. The transport also had to be maintained of course. Heavy-goods-lorry drivers did not need a licence and it was not uncommon for one lorry to pull four trailers, with a driver and a mechanic on board and not very efficient lighting. The driving and steering of such steam lorries was very complicated and in 1936 the matter was discussed in the House of Commons and House of Lords under The Road Traffic Act 1936, and showmen's vehicles were discussed at length.

> ... travelling showmen's vehicles which go from fair to fair. These engines have been made for some three-quarters of a century and are of a somewhat antiquated design in many cases and it requires two men to drive and steer these vehicles ... on these vehicles there is, first of all, a driver. He is, in fact, an engineer. He is the man who is responsible for getting up steam, applying the brakes and generally looking after the firing and mechanical side of the engines ... at the same time he is giving the necessary signals to the men behind on different trailers. They can pull three enormous trailers and a watering cart, a train of five vehicles travelling along the road. Under this new act he would continue to have a licence. ... The man who steers the vehicles is the steersman. He is the man who actually turns the small wheels which direct the front wheels of the vehicle. ... if the clause goes through as it stands at the moment he will not need a licence. Anyone will be able to steer – a lunatic, or a half-wit, or even the fat lady in the show [freak shows on fairgrounds] if she is able to get into the small space available. On the other hand, of course, you could have the driver who goes round 'The Walls of Death'. These vehicles only go 5 miles an hour. ... People affected by the Bill, the showmen, have been trying to get the Minister of Transport to accept their view about the proposed new regulation. ... The Act proposed that steersmen should also take out a driving licence. ... These vehicles cost £2000–£3000 and owners would not let anyone steer who was not competent. The age limit was 21 – apparently it was mostly coconut shy owners who were steersmen.

The amendment to the Bill to make it compulsory for the steersmen of a travelling showman's vehicle to have a licence was withdrawn.[4]

Negotiating these vehicles to and from fairgrounds was not an easy matter either, especially on narrow, winding country roads. Usually a member of the team would survey the route beforehand to find the most convenient route. On top of which there was the fee of £5 for a driving licence. Diesel-run lorries replaced steam lorries from about 1933 onwards.

In 1939 the Wall of Death rider 'Fearless Egbert' wrote an article in *The Leyland Journal* called 'Carrying around a Wall of Death' describing in some detail the transporting of walls. It was then reported in *The World's Fair*.[5]

The wall itself, eight motorcycles, his Wall of Death car, and a caged lion were transported on two Leyland lorries and their trailers. Owners preferred old Leylands (1914 and on) because they were cheaper and had good chassis. Up to 2,000 miles a year was an average mileage for a wall travelling the UK. Each lorry carried five to six tons with six tons on the trailer. The lorries also ran when on site, being fitted with dynamos which ran for 30–40 hours a week, providing lighting for the show.

Putting up and taking down a wall was hard work. Firstly the ground had to be perfectly flat, which entailed a lot of work on uneven muddy fairgrounds. Then a circle was marked out with the centre point found, a crucial aspect, and eighteen wooden sleepers were put down in a circle, on top of which the eighteen-piece circular floor was laid. Then the eighteen very heavy vertical panels were erected and bolted together on the outside. The banking on the interior and the central pole came next, and the interior safety cable, walkround and handrails were then added. The steps from the ground to the walkround were then put together and finally the bally was erected, together with the painted bally back and the ticket office. Lighting then had to be installed, run by a generator.

Maintaining the bikes was absolutely crucial – tyres had to be regularly checked for damage and pressure. They always had to have in stock new tyres, in case of blow-outs. Oil levels had to be maintained. Very important was inspecting a bike after a crash, to identify and repair any damage.

The wall itself had to be regularly checked so see whether there was any damage, which could affect the ride or be a safety hazard for the riders and the public.

A rider used his/her own bike. Although some other bikes were used, like the Rex Acme, most riders preferred the American 1920s 600cc Indian Scout.

What riders liked was a side footplate 4 inches wide, on which they could stand to perform some of their tricks. Indian Scouts were light, fast and very, very reliable, and the front leaf spring was useful on which to place a foot to ease moving over the handlebars (to do tricks). Riders customized their bikes by removing unnecessary parts, like headlights and

Indian Scout poster (copyright the Baer family Library)

the front mudguard, and adjusting other parts of the bike. Parts and bikes were also available in the UK.

For more detailed technical reasons why riders liked this bike see Allan Ford and Nick Corble's second book, *You can't wear out an Indian Scout*,[6] so called because of the advertising in America which stated:

> You can't wear out an Indian Scout,
> or its brother the Indian Chief.
> They're built like rocks to stand hard knocks,
> it's the Harleys that cause the grief.

Needless to say the advertising was spot-on – many of these original 1920s bikes are still in use today on walls, ninety-five years after they were made.

Another poem said: 'If I had a Harley, I'd leave it for a thief / And with the insurance, I'd buy an Indian Chief'.[7]

A variety of tricks were performed by trick riders, but not all riders did tricks, some only did straight rides. A rider would ride round the top of the wall, just below the safety cable. Another trick was to take a pillion rider on the front handlebars.

The Hell Drivers Race saw two or three riders racing each other on the wall, overtaking each other. Dips of Death – where a rider, and sometimes two at a time, rode up to just below the safety cable and did a 90°turn then rode almost to the banking below, and up again, time and time again.

Indian Shop London poster

Trick riders could sit on the handlebars, steering with their legs; put one leg over the handlebar and have their arms in the air; stand up on the foot rest with their arms in the air; sit side-saddle on the tank; sit backwards with their arms in the air. Some riders rode blindfolded, and one of the most spectacular was for one rider to tow another on roller skates. The most difficult, which few performed, was two bikes on the wall riding round in different directions (this caused at least two deaths).

From 1929 onwards some riders also drove cars on the wall. These were usually Austin 7s, which were light, readily available, fairly cheap and, once adapted, suitable for driving on a wall. All drivers adapted the cars by removing items which were not necessary, like lights and mudguards.

Several showmen owned and toured walls during this period, including Anderson and Rowland, Pat and John Collins, the Codona family in Scotland, Billy Butlin, Mark Lloyd, the Grants, Elias Harris, Eddie Monte, Albert Evans Senior, the Wards, the Perrys, Tornado Smith, Jack North, the Skinners, Jack Barry, and my family: George, Jack, Bob and Frank Todd and Wyn and Gladys Soutter.

Early on, some of the public thought the Wall of Death was a fake, the riders somehow attached to magnets, and called for it to be banned. At least a dozen women fainted when watching the show.

Because of the perceived danger in riding a wall insurance was either impossible to get or extremely expensive. So at the end of each performance on a wall the spieler told the audience this and encouraged them to throw coins into the bottom of the wall. This money was known as 'Nobbins', which had to be collected after each show. At the end of, say, a week's performances, a considerable amount of coins had been collected so owners had to have especially large bank bags in which to bank the coins. The total received was divided between the riders. There was quite often a stooge who threw coins in first.

Fairs were extremely popular at that time – there were 250 fairs each week throughout Britain. Some were very large – Newcastle Town Moor was the biggest in Europe; Oxford St. Giles, Nottingham Goose Fair, Cambridge Mid-Summer and King's Lynn Mart were also very large. There were also smaller ones and even smaller ones, called back-end fairs, which took place after the summer season.

There were no paid holidays and those who did go on holiday stayed in B and B and had to leave the premises all day, so they had plenty of time to enjoy themselves. Thousands of people attended the large fairs and the Wall of Death had plenty of competition on any fairground. There were the large rides owned by the Riding Masters, such as dodgems, the Skid, Mont Blanc, the Big Dipper, the Walzer, Loch Ness Monster, Brooklands Speedway, Boxing booths, African villages, Moon Rocket, the Octopus, Divebomber, Autodrome, helter skelter, shooting galleries, darts, ping-pong stalls, and carousels, all brightly painted and with plenty of noise to attract the crowd, including fairground organs. Along with the rides there were also a variety of shows, including Bostock and Wombwell's Menageries, with animals from all over the world; Al Capone's armoured

Nottingham Goose Fair from the air

car; Dare-Devil Peggy High Diver; fortune tellers; Prof. Brodie, who used electric voltage to produce sparks on himself; a large variety of freak shows, which could include midgets, fat ladies, very tall people, India rubber men, Fasting Ladies, Bearded Ladies, albinos, and snake charmers. My grandfather showed a Fasting Lady show which was very popular. There were also children's rides and prizes like goldfish, caged birds and toys.

Riders employed by wall owners usually slept in digs. Once a rider owned a wall they usually bought a caravan. By 1929 there was one caravan builder/repairer in the North and showmen from all over the country used him, although second-hand caravans were also widely available. Riding Masters had very elaborate and expensive living wagons, with beautiful carving, cut-glass in the interior, separate bedrooms and open fires. They were towed from fair to fair by large tractors or trucks. A reporter described a typical interior:

> To the average person the interior of a first-class caravan would undoubtedly constitute a revelation. Bright and cheery looking oil lamps swing out from obscure corners, a seemingly blank wall reveals itself at a touch as a cupboard or wardrobe, whilst at the pull of a handle a neat little 'table' emerges from its place of concealment. One of the chief features of a modern caravan is its cooking stove, which in one instance had every part of it electroplated. The windows are usually of heavy plate glass and are veiled with bright and dainty curtains and the caravan generally 'wears a dust coat' to shield its varnish from both sun and rain.[8]

---

1. *Somerset and West of England Advertiser*, 17 October 1930 (reproduced with kind permission of the British Newspaper Archive, www.britishnewspaperarchive.co.uk).
2. Allan Ford and Nick Corble, *Riding the Wall of Death*. Tempus Publishing, 2006.
3. *The World's Fair*, 29 June 1929.
4. Hansard, House of Commons, 8 May 1936, Vol 311 xx2070-82.
5. *The World's Fair*, 22 July 1939.
6. Allan Ford and Nick Corble, *You Can't Wear Out an Indian Scout*. Amberley Publishing, 2009.
7. Tod Rafferty, *The Indian – The History of a Classic American Motorcycle*. Bramley Books, 1998.
8. *The Lincolnshire Standard and Boston Guardian*, 10 May 1930 (reproduced with kind permission of the British Newspaper Archive, www.britishnewspaperarchive.co.uk).

Chapter 2

The Thorny Question of the First Wall of Death in the UK

The first mention of a Wall of Death in Europe appears to be in 1907 in France. That year The Great Peking–Paris [motor car] Race took place. One of the participants was Charles Godard, who was accompanied by the French journalist Jean du Taillis. The same year du Taillis wrote a book about the race and mentions that Godard was a Wall of Death rider at the Mardi Gras in Montparnasse. In 1964 Allen Andrews also wrote a book called *The Mad Motorists* about the race in which he mentions the Wall of Death three times. His source was a close friend of Godard. Whether this was a real vertical Wall of Death or similar to a German *Todesfahrt* we will probably never know. *Todesfahrt* is the German word for Wall of Death.

Die Todesfahrt

The first vertical Silodrome (Wall of Death) in America was at Coney Island, New York in 1915. In the UK in 1924 at the British Empire Exhibition there was a 'Death Ring', probably something like *Die Todesfahrt.*

> For those who enjoy watching thrills, the 'Death Ring' provides of the best, since in this cup-shaped steel cage a motorcyclist, and sometimes three, ride around the top of the track in a horizontal position and parallel to the ground.[1]

In April 1929 Sir Malcolm Campbell, whilst in South Africa trying to break the world speed record in his car, saw a Wall of Death in Johannesburg. The 1929 poster advertising the Wall of Death at the Kursaal, Southend, in June 1929, quotes him as saying in South Africa regarding the wall, 'I have never seen its equal in all my life'.[2] For many years, people have been debating, and still are, when the first Wall of Death appeared in the UK, through letters to *The World's Fair,* and it has also been discussed and researched by Wall of Death historians and journalists: Phil Samson, motoring journalist of the *Daily Telegraph,* and Wall of Death historians Allan Ford, Alan Mercer, Nick Corble, Neil Calladine and Ned Williams.

The aim of this chapter is to set out the correct date, as I see it, following my research.

The British newspaper *The World's Fair* was first published in Oldham, England, in 1904 and is still published today. In the 1930s it had a large circulation (but no figures are available), cost 3d, was published weekly and was forty-eight pages long. It was, and still is, solely devoted to travelling showmen, fairgrounds, amusement parks, circuses and magicians, together with a supplement about market traders. The reporting was very varied and included legal cases, obituaries, birthdays, engagements, marriages and deaths. The Showmen's Guild also regularly reported in the paper. It also had a letters page.

Several local amateur reporters wrote weekly columns about fairs in their area, which, in some cases, were very detailed. Such reports would list which showmen were present at a fair, which rides, games, shows and children's rides. In many cases there would be dozens of showmen and shows present. Comments were sometimes added about how busy the fair had been, how many of the public had visited, and often included interviews with showmen. However, not all of the UK had such reporters and the South of England, London and Scotland had very few reports.

The paper also gave weekly listings of all the fairs in the UK in that week – as has already been stated there were often 250 a week. All showmen bought this weekly paper as did members of the public, since fairs were so popular.

Continental showmen also bought the paper and used it to advertise for riders to ride abroad, e.g. in Spain, Germany and even Bermuda, or to buy or sell walls, and Continental riders used it to try and get work in the UK.

The paper had a large selection of commercial adverts, which varied from the new rides and equipment available to goods available as prizes for fairground games. Trade fairs, exhibitions and new inventions were also featured.

However, the private advertisement columns contained a wealth of information from July 1929 on the Wall of Death and it is very clear that the paper was the major form of communication between wall owners, wall riders, Riding Masters seeking wall riders, amusement parks seeking walls with riders etc. A 1930s photo in my collections shows three Wall of Death riders reading *The World's Fair* and I suspect it is an article about them.

Three Wall of Death riders reading *The World's Fair*, 1930s

It should be remembered that very few people had telephones. To start with such adverts were in the 'circus' column but the editors soon realized – or were told! – that the Wall of Death was not a circus and a new column headed 'Dromes' was created. Not all advertisers used their names but gave a *World's Fair* box number. I suspect this was to hide details from competitors or it might simply have been because riders and owners were constantly moving round the country from week to week. The Post Office, however, did offer a special delivery service to showmen – if they had post for a showman who had moved on, they forwarded the post to the next fair. Sometimes an advert was quite personal, e.g. could a rider (name given) please contact so and so (name given) a prospective employer. Adverts also included those who wanted to buy or sell a wall.

As far as the Wall of Death was concerned the paper, partly but not completely, charted its introduction into the UK. One problem was that not all local reporters named whose wall was at a particular fair or named the riders. A typical entry might say at such and such a fair 'a Wall of Death was present'. Secondly, reporters who actually named riders sometimes got their nationality wrong. Canadian riders were said to be American and even some British riders were occasionally reported as being American. This happened to my British mother. Of course the general press also reported on the Wall of Death.

The matter of when the first wall appeared in the UK was still being debated in 1975 when George Purser from Ramsgate, Kent, wrote to *The World's Fair* stating that he worked as a spieler-mechanic for a wall owned by Silodrome Pty in 1928 on Ramsgate seafront. According to him the riders were Cyclone Jack Cody, Captain Bob and Marion Perry.[3]

He also wrote to me saying that he worked for that wall in 1928. Unfortunately the letter to *The World's Fair* influenced the wall's history thereafter, and to this day. For instance the Dingles Fairground Heritage Centre in Devon held a celebration of the Wall of Death in 2008, advertising it as the 80th anniversary – 1928–2008.

In order to clarify George Purser's letter I recently researched all the local Ramsgate and Thanet newspapers of the time and there was absolutely no mention of a wall or Silodrome in Ramsgate in 1928. There were, however, two references to a wall appearing in July 1930.

On 11 July 1930, there was an article on 'Dare Devil Riders – Ramsgate's Super Thrill appearing at the Harbour Site, Ramsgate' which included a long description of the riders, Captain Bob Perry and his sister, Dare-Devil Marion Perry (historians think this couple were married but it was thought the public might find it more exciting if the riders were single). This article was given considerable prominence in the paper, and was two columns long.

> In the final act, Bob and Marion took the wall together and crossed and re-crossed in an amazing fashion – then Bob gave us a display of the Dips of Death, of which he is the originator.[4]

Carolus, who wrote a weekly column in *The Advertiser*, also referred to his visit to the Wall of Death, which he found thrilling, although he declined to go up as a pillion rider. Headed 'A Real Thrill', in it he commented 'I have never seen a more thrilling spectacle'.

Cyclone Jack Cody is not mentioned but he quite probably joined the act later in the season. An advert in the newspaper publicized this wall being at Merrie England in 1930, with Capt. Bob Perry (the originator of the Dips of Death) and Dare-Devil Marion Perry, America's Greatest Woman Stunt Rider.[5] It would seem clear that had a wall appeared in 1928, this newspaper would have reported on it.

Regarding George Purser's letters, the Perrys and Cyclone Jack Cody all arrived in the UK in June 1929.[6]

Even more evidence can be seen by reading the 1929 flyer relating to Capt. Bob Perry, Cyclone Jack Cody and Plucky Jennie Perry appearing at the Kursaal in Southend-on-Sea, in late June 1929, presented by Silodrome Pty Ltd: 'For the first time in Europe, after Touring the World, America's latest and greatest of all thrillers the Wall of Death – a Silodrome built at an angle of 90 degrees has been conquered.'[7]

From this published flyer it is clear, therefore, that the Perrys and Cyclone Jack Cody were not at Ramsgate in 1928 but in 1930 and it looks as if George Purser's recollection was incorrect.

Kelvin Hall in Glasgow had long been a centre for amusements and Albert Evans Junior (ex-Wall of Death rider/owner) told me that his father Albert Evans Senior remembered seeing a Silodrome at Kelvin Hall in 1928. However, the earliest report in Scottish newspapers I can find about a wall at Kelvin Hall was December 1929, when it was reported that 'a new feature of the carnival this year is the Wall of Death'.[8] So it would appear that Albert Evans Senior also got his date wrong.

The first Wall of Death in the UK referred to in *The World's Fair* was 8 June 1929, when it was reported that Billy Ward and his wife gave a display at Manchester, Belle Vue. By 29 June Cyclone Jack Cody appeared with the Perrys at the Kursaal in Southend. After the first 8 June 1929 short report, a longer 29 June report appeared in *The World's Fair* on the wall at the Kursaal, entitled 'The Wall of Death The Very Latest Thrill at Southend':

> Here men and women actually ride motorcycles at breakneck speed on the side of a perfectly straight-up wall, and defy the ordinary laws of gravity to make them fall. Moreover, they not only ride but do tricks whilst in this perilous position. They at times take not only their hands off the handle-bars, but their legs off the pedals also, meantime they gavotte and skylark about whilst on the wall seemingly as they wish.

The article then goes on to describe the wall in detail and further comments: 'Words can hardly express what you feel like as you come away from ten minutes of this'.[9]

So it would appear that the first wall was in Manchester, June 1929, and not in Ramsgate or Southend. In July 1929, the first photographs of a wall appeared in *The World's Fair.* At this stage the paper did not print many photographs but most of those they did print were of a wall. *The World's Fair* annual review of the year 1929 stated 'the only real novelty has been the arrival of an exhibition ride known as the Wall of Death and later by many [other] descriptive names'.[10]

Had this not been the case I feel that a rider would have written to correct the report since riders were always very quick to correct any Wall of Death reports in the paper. It is also noteworthy that George Purser did not challenge this statement. As a member of the Showmen's Guild he would, no doubt, have taken the paper.

The newspaper was not the only record of the walls. In 1929 the Italian artist Alfredo Ortelli clearly went to London and produced a lovely Italian poster illustrating four riders on the wall and one on the base, with the Italian words 'London is the home of a new motorcycling act, there is a circular velodrome, where a woman on a motorcycle speeds round from top to bottom'.

Un numero arretrato Cent. 80

ILLUSTRAZIONE DEL POPOLO

Sedici pagine - Centesimi 40

Londra si appassiona per un nuovo genere di corsa con la motocicletta. Sei motociclisti, tra cui una donna, girano vorticosamente su un muro circolare eretto in un velodromo: le macchine e i corpi sono paralleli al suolo.

Italian Wall of Death poster, 1929 (copyright the Mary Evans Picture Library)

All that said, Alan Mercer, Wall of Death historian, has recently found a reference in *The Register News-Pictorial*, Adelaide, which shows a photograph of and reference to 'The Wall of Death – a racing motorcyclist on an English track, speeding round a perpendicular cylindrical wall 96 feet in circumference – a track termed "the Wall of Death"'. This was dated 22 January 1929. The short description does not say the wall was in England. So far Alan has been unable to find any further information. Personally I have concluded that this English track was probably South African, where the wall had been introduced earlier in the 1920s.

---

1. *British Empire Exhibition 1924*, p. 100.
2. *Essex Life Magazine*, February 2007, article by Nick Corble.
3. *The World's Fair*, 1975, week not known.
4. *The Advertiser*, 11 July 1930.
5. Ibid., 18 July 1930.
6. Ancestry.com.
7. 'The Kursaal Flyers', *Essex Life*, February 2007, article by Nick Corble.
8. *Dundee Evening Telegraph*, 3 December 1929 (reproduced with kind permission of the British Newspaper Archive, www.britishnewspaperarchive.co.uk).
9. *The World's Fair*, 29 June 1929, p. 30.
10. Ibid., 4 January 1930.

Chapter 3

Wall of Death Riders invade Britain – 1929–1930s

By 1929 the Wall of Death had been developed in America, where it was known as the Silodrome. It was also touring South Africa and Continental Europe at that time. Allan Ford's book *Riding the Wall of Death* precisely and interestingly charts its development from speedway racing on the flat to riding a motorbike on a vertical wall.

Late in 1929 several American, Canadian and South African riders came to England. In the USA the Great Depression had started and many amusement parks were closing down so there was less opportunity for riders to get work, and since there were about 100 walls there competition was great. Also very significantly the Wall Street Crash took place in October 1929 so I do not think it is a coincidence that riders left the USA for other countries.

Some of those who came over to the UK in December 1929 were Louis C. Shwarootz, his brother Jack Cody, and Oliver A. Roland and his wife; and on 13 December 1929, Samuel and Mrs Anderson and Robert Ernest Restall, a Canadian, aged 24. Bob Perry (American) and Jenny Perry had arrived and Joe Silverstone (South African) arrived in June 1929.

In May 1930 Robert Restall's two brothers, Goldwin C. Restall aged 20 and William A. Restall aged 18, arrived. In December 1930 Ferald Eugene Egbert (thereafter known as Fearless Egbert) arrived. He had previously toured on the Continent and I suspect had met the showman Pat Collins there, who might have persuaded him to come to the UK.

All these men and women were experienced Wall of Death riders and the Restall brothers, Louis C. Shwarootz, Oliver A. Roland, Joe Silverstone and Ferald Eugene Egbert were to have a very long-lasting and profound influence on all my Soutter and Todd family members for the rest of their lives.

In the 1930s there were more American and South African riders coming over but this book is only concerned with the ones who were connected to my family.

By 18 December, only five days after the arrival of Robert Restall, Gladys Soutter, my British aunt, was riding as a pillion passenger on a motorcycle at the Derby Xmas Fair, on the 'Wizards on the Wall'. By 27 December Samuel Anderson, Mrs Anderson and Robert Restall were also riding the wall at the Derby Fair.

How on earth did these young men and women manage to be riding and touring so quickly after their arrival, along with British riders whom they had trained?

By 1929, there were several companies and organizations with offices in London. The American Silo-Drome Riders Association was at 10 Furnival Mansions, Wells Street, London W.1. Their large trade card stated it was 'A Combination of America's best speed exponents on a Vertical Wall'. Specialities were 'High Speed Motorcycle and Automobile Riding', 'Trick and Acrobatic Stunts on a Vertical Wall' and 'Each rider is unanimously praised by the world's press', and there was a sketch of a man riding a wall with the audience watching.

American Silo-Drome Riders Association trade card

The two directors of this association were Sam M. Naishtad and Billy Ward, and all communications were to be addressed to the Managing Director, Sam M. Naishtad. There is no telephone number but it should be realized that in those days if you posted a letter by 9 a.m. it would be received by lunch time, if it was local, the next day if not local, with several deliveries per day.

Naishtad was born in Odessa, Russia, in 1896. It appears that aged only 14 he worked himself round the world and ended up in South Africa, where he joined the army. In 1919, with other showmen, he founded the Showmen's Guild of South Africa.[1] He left South Africa and was in Belfast, Northern Ireland, where he ran a company call The Star Amusement Company.[2]

Sam Naishtad

He appears to have come to the UK in 1929 and by then was the UK representative of the famous 75-year-old German showman Hugo Hess, who presided over many Continental fairgrounds and owned a factory, where he built showground rides. Naishtad appears to have spent several years in Germany since he was involved with amusements there and by 1931 was a Continental Riding Master and had been responsible for introducing the Wall of Death to the Continent from South Africa. By 1931 he owned so many walls on the Continent that he sold them all, for a large profit. Also during that time he went to Cairo, where he was responsible for the large Cairo Exhibition, and on his return to the UK he was also involved in the newly created White City Amusement Park. He spoke six languages and was reported to be a very nice man. In England he became very friendly with John Collins and Jack Barry, Riding Masters, and the three of them were known to fairground people as The Three

Musketeers, because they were frequently seen together on fairgrounds, working out which ride would be situated where.[3]

In 1933 a photo of Naishtad and Pat Collins appeared on the front page of *The World's Fair* with the caption 'Two Well-Known Showmen'.[4]

At the same time as being the Managing Director of The American Silo-Drome Riders Association, he was also working for Morgan Hastings in London. They had offices at 42 Sussex Place, London, SW7 and a garage in Putney. They marketed chassis made by Stewart Motor Corporation in Buffalo, New York, and since chassis was also the word used for motorcycles they were probably importing these as well. According to my mother Morgan Hastings also built walls in the UK and very fine ones at that. By 1931 they also had a garage in Yeovil, Somerset, and were still in existence in London in 1939.

Several of the wall riders coming to the UK in 1929–1930 put Morgan Hastings down as their address in the UK.

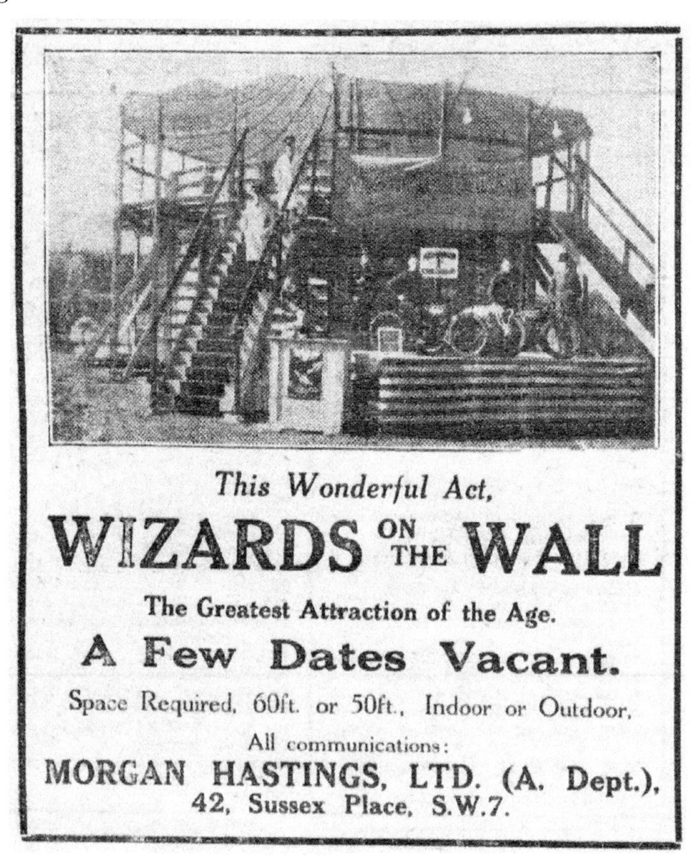

Wizards on the Wall advertisement – *The World's Fair*, 26 October 1929

In October 1929, Morgan Hastings Ltd. put a large advert in The World's Fair, which indicated that they did have their own walls: 'This Wonder Act Wizards on the Wall, The Greatest Attraction of the Age. A Few Dates Vacant. Space required 60 foot or 50 foot indoor or outdoor', accompanied by a photograph of one of their walls.

They were also supplying riders. By May 1930 they had eight walls on tour, one of which was unusual in that it could cope with very large audiences, and was therefore bigger than normal.[5]

Naishtad managed the newly arrived riders, several of whom knew each other anyway. By managing he found pitches for the wall, organized the advertising in local papers, had leaflets and posters printed for each venue (and there were many all over the country), arranged travel and transport of riders and the walls and was in charge of publicity. He arranged which riders were going to ride with whom and where. He was also a journalist and in the early days there are several newspaper reports where he describes the wall and what the riders do on the walls. He was clearly well liked by the riders and very successful and was still managing riders as late as 1939 (my parents until 1938 and Fearless Egbert until 1939).

There was also a company called Silodrome (Proprietary) Ltd., a South African company. They were responsible for the much-trumpeted early show at the Kursaal Amusement Park in Southend in June 1929. I don't know whether this company was an off-shoot of the American Silo-Drome Riders Association. In an article in *The World's Fair* the director C. More stated that his company had contracted with twelve of the World's best 'Death Riders', six of whom had come to the UK.[6]

The American Amusement Company was also in London (see Allan Ford's book). It is not clear whether this company was anything to do with Naishtad's Star Amusement Company.

A British company, Orton and Spooner, had also built ten walls in 1929.

The American Silo-Drome Riders Association, The American Amusement Company and Morgan Hastings were looking to train and employ riders and the latter published adverts etc.

So these walls already existed in England in 1929 and were ready to be ridden. Plenty of riders had arrived and British ones were being trained by the ones who had arrived.

The new 'American craze' was about to explode across Britain. By July 1930 it was such a craze that it was used in a political cartoon. Stanley Baldwin, then the ex-Prime Minister, is seen riding a car on a wall with the words 'Food Taxes', 'Tariff Wall' and 'Safeguarding'.[7]

The letters column in *The World's Fair* also started to print letters about walls, usually from wall managers. It would seem that all sorts of riders

The Political Wall of Death, 26 July 1930 (reproduced with kind permission of The British Newspaper Archive, www.britishnewspaperarchive.co.uk)

were trying to claim to have been the first rider in the UK. Joe Silverstone corrected a previous letter which had claimed Sam Anderson to be the first rider, and pointed out that Billy and Margie Ward were the first in Manchester, June 1929. Sam Anderson could not have been the first rider because he did not arrive in the UK until December 1929. Unfortunately in this letter Silverstone calls managers 'flattie managers'. The term flattie was used by show people to indicate people not members of the guild and was rather an insult.[8]

Thereafter letters from various managers became quite acrimonious. The following week Roy Arthur, a manager of Wizards on the Wall, denied that he had said Sam Anderson was the first rider. The same week Sam Naishtad wrote in, firstly complaining about being called a flattie, suggesting that he had been a showman long before Silverstone, and then pointing out that Silverstone was a flattie. He also pointed out that he had founded the Showmen's Guild of South Africa in 1919. He then issued a challenge for Silverstone and Roy Arthur to give a speech inside or outside a wall. Naishtad would adjudicate, and give the winner his first-class rail fare and £25 towards his expenses. It is not known whether this challenge was taken up.

In 1931 letters were about the noise walls made on fairgrounds. Once again Roy Arthur had written in complaining about them. A. St. Clair Hutchings replied saying that Arthur knew very little about fairground work. There was plenty of noise on fairs from walk-ups, drums, trumpets, klaxons and fairground organs.[9]

By 1932 the topic was 'Wall Riding Feats'. Once again Arthur had written in with detrimental remarks about British riders and the fact that they were not such good trick riders as Americans. Johnnie Parr, British Wall of Death rider, who had ridden with my mother at the 1930 Oktoberfest, replied pointing out that 90 per cent of British riders were competent at trick riding. He suggested that Arthur had never heard of the by then famous British riders, listing at least fourteen. He then asked whether Arthur had heard about the Todd brothers, who did a roller-skating act on the wall, and asked if Arthur could list any trick which British riders could not do. Had he also not heard of the 16-year-old girl rider (my mother) who does all the motorcycle tricks which were done by the American riders and who, although taught to ride straight by an American (Canadian actually) learned all the tricks herself? According to Parr most of the Americans learned their trick riding in the UK.[10]

---

1. Letter from Sam Naishtad, *The World's Fair*, 5 July 1930.
2. eBay stamped envelope.
3. *The World's Fair*, 28 November 1933.
4. Ibid., 27 May 1933.
5. Ibid. 31 May 1930 and 14 June 1930.
6. Ibid., 13 July 1929.
7. *The Sheffield Daily Independent*, 26 July 1930 (reproduced with kind permission of the British Newspaper Archive, www.britishnewspaperarchive.co.uk).
8. *The World's Fair*, 28 June 1930.
9. Ibid., 21 March 1931.
10. Ibid., 5 November 1932.

Chapter 4

John Todd, My Uncle, Known as Jack

Born: 1904, Weymouth, UK. Married: Iris Dorothy Collins, 1932 (divorced by 1948). Died: 1989. No children.

Riding names: briefly as Fearless Jack, briefly as Jack and Jill (Jill Desmond), Speedy Todd, The Original Death Rider and thereafter Jack Todd.

Rode from 1929 until 1950. Owned own wall from late 1930 to 1950.

Uncle Jack, my father's brother, was one of several uncles, all of whom were riders and owners, three of whom were Todds. He was quite a character with a good sense of humour, always relating interesting stories, and very cheerful, and he and I got along very well.

Aged 16 he was employed by my grandfather in Folkestone, Kent, learning the antique and exchange and mart business. By about 1925 the family were living in Whitstable, Kent, and Jack was well known locally, by the police!, for riding his motorbike along Herne Bay seafront. My grandfather had been an auctioneer in Birmingham but later became an antique dealer and a showman with small side stalls. As such he would have taken *The World's Fair.* On 8 June 1929, it contained an article on a 'Thrilling Motorcycle Act' – the first report in the paper about a Wall of Death.[1] I am certain that as a keen motorcyclist, Jack would have read this article and realized that he could also do this and approached the showman Pat Collins.

Pat Collins was born in the mid-nineteenth century and by the early twentieth century he was a famous showman running many fairgrounds and fairs and a large number of rides. He was one of the first British showmen to realize the potential of both the Wall of Death and the Globe of Death, although he himself was not a rider. Collins' wall was initially called The Wall of Death but the company Silodromes Ltd. had registered the name and they took Collins to court and won.[2] So Collins had to choose another name. His ride was called the 'Death Riders', or 'Drome of Satan'. However, the term death riders was often used thereafter in general to describe Wall of Death riders, regardless who they worked for.

Jack was the first of my Todd family to be reported on in newspapers as riding the wall. In 1931, after letters to *The World's Fair* about walls, he wrote in calling the whole correspondence on Death Rides a 'silly controversy', and stating that he was the first Death Rider in the country (he meant British rider), stating that he had been riding for three years and now owned his own drome.[3]

By September 1929, he was touring the UK riding with two others on Collins' wall. Even at that early stage it would seem Pat Collins was certainly keen to promote the new show, for Jack appeared at Dudley Carnival, Leeds, King's Lynn, Oxford St. Giles, Walsall, Leicester, Hull, Loughborough and Birmingham Onion Fair. In October they appeared at the famous Nottingham Goose Fair, where it was reported: 'the latest attraction the Wall of Death was without a doubt the greatest sensation of the present century and has been the talk of Nottingham.'[4]

At Birmingham Onion Fair it was reported that 'the Death Defiers, Williams, Stanford and Todd appeared in their thrilling motor cycling, within a perpendicular tube 20 feet high and 40 feet in diameter, dashing around on motorcycles'.[5]

At the North East Coast Exhibition in December 1929, the Wall of Death drew 150,000 people to see it, although I do not know whose wall it was.[6]

In 1998 a Jack Patten wrote to me saying he had seen his first wall at King's Lynn in 1929 and 'to me it is the premier fairground show, never to be surpassed'. So sixty-nine years later he still remembered it.

At the beginning of 1930 The World's Fair reported 'the only real novelty in 1929 was the exhibition ride known as the Wall of Death and later by many descriptive names'.[7]

So Jack was one of the earliest British riders if not the earliest. Since he was already an accomplished motorcyclist I think he probably taught himself to ride.

By 1930 Jack was Pat Collins' principal rider and spent the whole year touring Britain with his wall. He was, amongst other places, at Oldham, Oxford St. Giles, Holbeck, Fazeley, Coventry, Birmingham Onion Fair, Burnley, Coleford, Sleaford, Montgomery, Chester Races Fair (where they had an audience of 19,000), Grantham and Nottingham Goose Fair.

At Shrewsbury in March it was reported:

> Last but decidedly not least, I must say the star attraction to Shrewsbury and district was certainly Collins' Drome of Death. The riders 'Fearless' Jack Todd and his charming wife give a wonderful exhibition of thrilling stunts on the wall – suffice to say that the main topic of conversation at the present time in Shrewsbury is the 'man who rides on the wall'.[8]

Such was the attraction at Grantham Fair that a poem was sent to the local paper:

We gathered in our thousands
To watch the Wall of Death
A spectacle so thrilling
That took away our breath
I took a car (two seater)
And hurtled round the track
Bang went another sixpence
Plus bruises on my back.[9]

Although one reporter called the wall a 'fearsome sounding name'.

At the July Burnley Fair:

> The Death Riders certainly affords as much thrill as the greatest sensation lover desires, as the motor cyclists ride around a perpendicular track at a big rate and perform dare-devilry which are hair-raising in the extreme.[10]

The wall was still touring at the end of the year when it appeared at Burnley Xmas Fair.

One of the Death Riders was a lady called Nita, who rode with Jack for some time. I was always under the impression that they married, and although I never met her I referred to her as my aunt, but I can find no marriage certificate. There is a family photo of Jack and Nita on the front of a wall, probably in 1929 or 1930 (shown on the next page). However, in my grandparents' house, over the fireplace, was an 8-foot-long rough piece of wood into which all the names of the family were burnt by poker – I distinctly remember Jack and Nita being on it. At Chester they were advertised as The Death Defiers in the Drome of Satan.

Jack and Jimmy Styles had a bad accident when the bike fell on both of them, resulting in Jack fracturing his skull, and they were rushed to hospital. The young rider was sitting on the front of the handlebars (perhaps Jack was teaching him) and swooned with dizziness, clutching at Jack, who tried, unsuccessfully, to hold him up. This news soon got around town and even more spectators paid to see the act.[11]

Jack and Nita, Death Riders, 1930

At Newport Fair Jack was riding with Jack Barry and Jill Desmond, reported as being his wife, although my family has never mentioned her and I cannot trace a marriage certificate. It was also mentioned that the reporter was surprised that Jack was riding so soon after his Chester accident.[12] The question of whether riders were single or married is curious, since some riders described themselves as married and they were not and some married women described themselves as single. Sometimes a married couple would even describe themselves as brother and sister. Perhaps it was perceived to be more glamorous if they were single. On the other hand reporters did not always get their facts correct.

Pat Collins' Death Riders metal admission token

At this stage paper tickets for entry to the wall were sometimes replaced by re-usable metal admission tokens. Collins had special ones made; on one side was printed 'Pat Collins Fair', on the other a skull and crossbones and the words 'Death Riders Admission'.

At the end of 1930 Jack left Pat Collins and bought his own wall and lorries to transport it. He called it 'Jack Todd's Ride of Death'. He was at Sheerness in August 1931, amongst other places, where he was advertised as 'Jack and Jill' (Jill Desmond).

The summer of 1932 was spent at Merrie England, Ramsgate, with his three brothers. This is covered in Chapter 11. At the end of the summer season Jack toured again and in September he appeared at Bartha Fair in Gloucestershire with his own wall, with one of his brothers, either Bob or George.

In the winter of 1932 Jack married Iris Dorothy Collins in London. I can find no evidence that Iris was a member of the famous Collins fairground family or that she was a Wall of Death rider or, in fact, whether she was Nita.

After 1932 Jack continued to travel his wall, including in Scotland, where two of his riders were the brothers Charlie and Ken Sirrell, both of whom came from Ramsgate, where Jack obviously met them.

In 1934 he placed an advert in *The World's Fair* announcing that his 'Original Drome of Thrills was open to propositions'. The Act consisted of car, roller skater and super motorcycle act. The roller skater was his brother Robert Todd. Jack called himself the 'Original Death Rider'.[13] In September he appeared at Uckfield Carnival Fair, together with an unnamed troupe of riders. His wall front had been repainted and decorated and he employed a Tannoy sound outfit. The Tannoy appears to have been a fairly new invention at the time and was probably advertised in *The World's Fair.* Meanwhile Charlie Sirrell was driving one of Jack's wall lorries in England and was fined by the local police on three counts – the lorry had no road licence, the back number plate was missing and he had no proper lights – what he did have alight was a candle in a glass jar! From 1925 Jack was also frequently in trouble with the law for not having a driving licence and even manufacturing a fake licence. He was also causing trouble for his three brothers as when he was taken to court and charged he often used one of their names. However, the Kent police at least soon worked out what he was doing. Thirty-five years later my father still remembered this and told the stories to my husband.

In 1935 Jack appeared at Clapham with a clever troupe of riders; at Chelmsford; at Barking Fete, advertised as 'Todd's Mighty Motordrome', so it probably included his brother Bob (on roller skates); and Willesden Hospital Carnival, Strood – where Jack called himself 'Speedy Todd'. At

Hastings Carnival, featuring a troupe of death riders and roller skaters, he sold 16,500 tickets. Thereafter he appeared at Stevenage, Barking Fete, Thame Horse Fair, Franklyn's Meadow and Poole.[14]

Jack Todd's 'Original Wall of Death' was the principal show at Folkestone, where Jack was also driving a car on the wall. He had come from Olympia, where he performed before the Prince of Wales.

By January 1936 he was looking for a team of wall riders and later in the year he was looking for a foreman.[15] By March he had probably engaged some Australian lady riders and was at Northampton. However, by April his brother Bob Todd returned from Italy, together with his wife Trude Todd, because at Luton he called the wall 'Todds' Wall of Death'. They then appeared at Wanstead Flats, Cambridge and Kettering. Appearing at Bedford Hospital Fair in August it was reported the fair had 80,000 visitors per day.[16] At the Birmingham Onion Fair on 24 September a report stated:

> In 1929 Jack Todd brought the first Wall of Death riders to the fair. This is his second visit and the riders were two Todd brothers and a Swiss girl. Before a full house the show began with a rider [sic] in which man and girl were on the same bike circling at break neck speed – and then the only roller-skating Wall of Death exponent in the world [not true there were a couple of others] and then Jack Todd drove a car round.[17]

The three appeared at Tamworth with the same act. In 1937 at Liverpool, 'Jack Todd executes sensational feats on the wall in a car plus there is a roller skater [Bob Todd]'.[18] Thereafter it is referred to as Todd's Wall of Death (which included brother Bob), appearing amongst other places at Blackheath and Thame – where 6,000 visited the fair in one day. At the Chester Races it was reported that Jack Todd executed sensational feats on the wall in a car, plus roller skating. By October the show had toured Sussex fairs and at Birmingham Onion Fair the show included five riders, Madcap Madge, Rob Roy, Signorita Trudy (Todd), Bob and Jack. They also appeared at Smethwick, Banbury and Birmingham again.

In 1938 at Exeter Easter Fair the show included roller skating by Bob and they had a lioness, which Jack took round.[19]

By May Jack managed to get a very important venue. He took his wall to the British Empire Exhibition in Glasgow. The exhibition ran from May until October and was opened by the King. More than 12 million people visited it. The official guide included a section 'All the Fun of the Fair' and stated:

The exhibition's amusement park is the finest in Britain and covers an area of sixteen acres. It contains the latest and greatest devices that human ingenuity can devise (including) the old Wall of Death, only this time a car rides the vertical wall – and carries passengers![20]

British Empire Exhibition, 1938

Jack Todd outside his Wall at British Empire Exhibition, Glasgow 1938

During the exhibition Jack, driving his car on the wall, had an accident and he and the car fell to the bottom, although Jack was not hurt. The wall was packed with an audience at the time.

Billy Butlin got the contract for all the amusements at the exhibition, so Jack's wall probably had Billy Butlin's name on it. I do have the official diagram of the exhibition, which clearly shows a Wall of Death, but have been unable to obtain any photographs of it, although I do have photos of Jack strolling round the exhibition. By May of 1938, only the first month, one million visitors had gone to the exhibition, so I have no doubt Jack made a lot of money.

In July 1939 he took his wall to the Liege International Water Exhibition for twelve weeks. The exhibition has 10 million visitors, and usually 600,000 on Sundays. Before and after that appearance he was also touring the UK, where he appeared in April at Allenton, Derbyshire.[21]

What he did during the war is in Chapter 18. After the war he continued to tour his wall and in 1948 he spent the season at Clarence Pier in Southsea, touring after that season finished. In the spring of 1949 he advertised: 'Wall riders with or without wall for exhibition in Teheran, Persia from February until May. Return air passage paid. English seasons to follow.'[22] So he took his wall to Teheran in Persia and on return continued to tour.

At the Festival of Britain he did not have his wall but he did have six shows in the fairground, including five live bears, which, apparently, were very popular. He had also bought Sir Malcolm Campbell's Blue Bird car, which he exhibited in the fairground.[23] Thereafter he retired to run an antique business in London, where he eventually died.

Unfortunately I have no idea whether he collected press cuttings or photos or what happened to them.

---

1. *The World's Fair*, 8 June 1929.
2. Ibid., 14 December 1929.
3. Ibid., 15 August 1931.
4. Ibid., 12 October 1929.
5. Ibid., 6 October 1929.
6. *Hartlepool Northern Daily Mail*, 16 December 1929 (reproduced with kind permission of the British Newspaper Archive, www.britishnewspaperarchive.co.uk).
7. *The World's Fair*, 4 January 1930.
8. Ibid., 29 March 1930.
9. *Grantham Journal*, 12 April 1930 (reproduced with kind permission of the British Newspaper Archive, www.britishnewspaperarchive.co.uk).

10. *Burnley News*, 12 July 1930 (reproduced with kind permission of the British Newspaper Archive, www.britishnewspaperarchive.co.uk).
11. *Hartlepool Northern Daily Mail*, 20 May 1930 (reproduced with kind permission of the British Newspaper Archive, www.britishnewspaperarchive.co.uk).
12. *The World's Fair*, 11 June 1930.
13. Ibid., 14 April 1934.
14. Ibid., 21 September 1935.
15. Ibid., 18 March 1936 and 1 March 1936.
16. Ibid., 15 August 1936.
17. Ibid., 3 October 1936.
18. Ibid., May 1937.
19. Ibid., April 1938.
20. British Empire Exhibition Official Guide.
21. *The World's Fair*, 22 April 1939.
22. Ibid., 4 January 1949.
23. Ibid., 28 June 1951.

Chapter 5
Robert Ernest Restall, My Uncle by Marriage

Born: Ontario, Canada, 1905. Married: Gladys Soutter, 1930.
Died: 1965 in Canada.
Son: Robert Leslie Restall, born 1931.
Riding names: Speedy Bob Lee, Speedy Lee, Bob Restall, Bob Lee.

By the time Robert Restall arrived in the UK from New York on 13 December 1929, aged 24, he was an experienced Wall of Death rider, one of the many riders who decided to try their luck in Europe. His address was given as c/o Morgan Hastings[1] but he lived in lodgings in the Old Kent Road, London.

The lodgings, principally for theatrical people, were owned by my great-grandmother. Also staying there was my aunt, Gladys Soutter, an actress. So the two met. As has been pointed out companies in London were already looking for young new British riders to train and clearly Robert told my aunt this. Robert worked for Morgan Hastings, who called their walls Wizards on the Wall. Aunt Gladys took up the challenge to learn to ride.

However, in the 1930s the term 'wizards on the wall' was also another general description of wall riders, even if they did not ride for Morgan Hastings. For instance, Pat Collins, who had his own walls, advertised in the 1930s for Wall Wizards or Death Riders.

By 17 December 1929, Gladys was at the Derby Xmas Fair, on Harry Hall's Fair Ground, being taught and riding as a pillion passenger on Suicide Jockey Roland's bike. Roland was another Morgan Hastings employee. The fair continued until 28 December. The *Derby Daily Telegraph* reported on several occasions on this new craze. The advert in the paper was headed 'Wizards on the Wall. The Wonder Thrill of the Age' and announced that they 'raced around a vertical wall at from 60 to 100 miles per hour, as seen by 30,000 persons weekly.'[2] These numbers were exaggerated since the speed is far too fast.

In fact a member of the public wrote to the newspaper pointing out that to reach 60 mph the motorcycle would have to do 60 laps on the wall per minute – and doubted that was possible.[3] This was not to be the only time that the reporting of such speeds was challenged. His letter is also interesting in that he points out that he had seen the show several times and as a motorcyclist himself he would like the opportunity to ride the wall.

The event was also written about in the same newspaper under 'Motordrome Riders Tilt with Death – this well-named Suicide Jockey Roland took with him as a passenger on the tank of a machine, a 21 year old girl, Miss Gladys Soutter, and both eventually rode taking their hands from the handlebars'.[4] (My aunt was in fact only twenty.) After Christmas Robert Restall had also arrived at the fair and was riding as Speedy Bob Lee, together with two other riders, Cyclone Anderson and on pillion occasionally Mrs Anderson. The Andersons had arrived in the UK on the same ship as Robert.

It was also reported that 'Dips of Death' were performed where the rider rides almost to the top of the wall and then dips down again, and he does this again and again. All in all they were hair-raising tricks and the reporter had never seen anything so thrilling. The wall was described as being 14 feet high and 30 feet in diameter and the riding display styled the 'Wall of Death', the riders spinning around the wall of wood – and trusting to luck and the momentum of the machine.

This was not the first wall to be ridden in the Midlands but it was the first Wizards on the Wall and the first Wizards Wall on which a member of my family rode.

By early 1930 Robert and Gladys were riding together, which is covered in Chapter 6.

---

1. Ancestry.co,uk
2. *Derby Daily Telegraph,* 17 December 1929 (reproduced with kind permission of the British Newspaper Archive, www.britishnewspaperarchive.co.uk).
3. Ibid., 30 December 1929.
4. Ibid., 18 December 1929.

Robert Restall and Gladys Soutter, 1930

Chapter 6
Gladys Marion Soutter, My Aunt

Born: 1909, Camberwell, London. Married: Robert Ernest Restall, 15 April 1930, Bristol. Widowed: 1965.

Son: Robert Leslie Restall, born 13 April, 1931, Penge, Kent.

Married: Jack Lancaster, 1974, Gloucester, UK. Died: 1982.

Riding names: Dare-Devil Gladys, Gladys Soutter. She rode the wall from December 1929 until about 1935 and owned her own wall in 1930s.

Her parents, my grandparents, were not wealthy at all – her father was an insurance agent. She had one sister and three brothers and her parents also brought up two other family children. So I suspect times were hard. Gladys at the age of 20 was a not-too-successful actress when she met Robert Restall in December 1929, and probably had never even heard of a Wall of Death. I was very close to my aunt and in her later life I often went to stay with her and Jack Lancaster.

Why would a young actress, who could not even ride a motorbike, take her life in her hands and offer to learn to ride the wall? She could have fallen in love with Robert at first sight!

Like so many other young girls who offered to learn to ride it offered a glamorous life and an opportunity to travel, and was certainly better paid than a waitress, telephone operator (as some of them were) or actress, who were looked down upon at the time.[1]

Life as a wall rider offered a chance of independence at a time when women were wanting more than becoming a housewife. Gladys was certainly plucky and as shown in the previous chapter within one week of meeting Robert she was riding pillion in the North of England on 18 December.

Very early in 1930 Gladys is also reported as riding pillion at Brixton – and quoted as 'The only English girl at the moment who has the requisite nerve to sit pillion on a machine racing round the vertical track at nearly 100 miles an hour' (she was not the only one and again the speed is exaggerated). The other riders were Curley Lou Cody and Suicide Jockey Rowlands, both American.[2] There will be more about Curley Lou Cody in the next chapter.

By 27 February 1930 Speedy Bob Lee, Gladys and Curley Cody were thrilling the crowds at Swindon, but by now Gladys was riding solo and was no longer a pillion rider; she also had adopted her riding name, Dare-Devil Gladys. A reporter wrote an article with the heading 'Wizards Scorn Danger'. He gave a good description:

> On arrival I found a large number of people gathered in front of the brilliantly illuminated round wooden structure, in front of which were eye-hitting signs, a platform on which stood an ear-splitting gentleman with megaphone and a couple of motor cycles periodically 'opening up' to provide the desired atmosphere. All this combined, no doubt, produced in me the irresistible temptation to pay my 'one and two pence' to see the show.

He then went on to describe the various rides, with the section on 'Dare-Devil Gladys' as follows:

> Miss Gladys Soutter was the next to take the wall. She was announced as Dare-Devil Gladys, and the only English girl who has the requisite nerve to ride the wall on the lightest British-made machine, which is a feature in itself. Beautiful Gladys, who is still in her teens, gave an exhibition of a 'Mile Time Trial'. Bob Lee and Curley Cody, riding parallel with each other, was a 'Spectacle that will remain impressed in my memory for years to come. ... I avail my readers themselves of this opportunity to go and see "The Wizards on the Wall"'.[3]

I do not know what the Mile Time Trial was and have never found it used again.

However, Gladys was never a really good rider and, according to my cousin Stuart Soutter, to start with the experienced riders only put enough petrol in the tank for the time she was on the wall, and when the petrol ran out Gladys HAD to bring the motorcycle down. Also she never learned to ride a motorcycle on the road. I also concluded that she was generally a straight rider and I have only ever seen one photo of her trick riding.

Later that week a tyre burst on Bob's bike and he was thrown into the centre of the wall and his bike landed on him. As he was unconscious for a while an ambulance was called but he refused to go to hospital, so Sam Naishtad (their Advance Manager) ordered a taxi and then took him to hospital. He was not seriously injured and was riding again the following night. A local reporter on hearing that Bob was riding again thought it was an advertising stunt and did not believe it and went down to see the show.[4]

On 1 April 1930 Gladys was riding the wall at the Red Cow Yard in Bedminster, again with Speedy Bob Lee and Curley Lou Cody. In the advert Gladys is billed as Dare-Devil Gladys. Ticket prices were 6d for adults and 3d for children. The show was there for a week and Speedy Bob Lee is also reported as taking young local ladies for a ride on the pillion. There was also a long newspaper report about the riders and an interview with Sam Naishtad, who also said that owing to the risks riders could not get insurance cover.[5]

Another newspaper report said:

> 'Speedy' Bob Lee and 'Curley' Cody are two American riders who have brought this 'pastime' to England. First the two were on the wall together in a daring 'pursuit' race; then 'Speedy' Bob went round standing on the foot rests and afterwards sitting side-saddle and with one foot over the handlebars. 'Curley' Cody's contribution to the thrills included similar tricks and an exhibition of the 'death dive' in which he climbs to the top of the wall and then shot down its shining surface with hair-raising rapidity. The reporter then had a pillion ride with Cody, becoming slightly dizzy. Curley reported that it took four months of practice before a rider could learn to overcome the air-pressure and do a 'straight' ride.[6]

The *Western Daily Press* also printed two photographs of Speedy Bob Lee on the wall.

The following week 8–15 April the three appeared for a week at Wildman's Ground, Gloucester. Again Speedy Bob Lee took a Bristol girl as a pillion passenger. The show continued to attract large crowds and paying customers. There was also an offer of a £50 reward for members of the public to ride the wall. A Mr Kilminster succeeded on a Rudge Motorbike and won £50, a considerable amount of money in those days.

A. W. Williams who had supplied the motorbike took advantage of this by announcing it in the newspaper – 'you can trust your life to a Rudge'.[7]

On 15 April 1930, just four months after they had met, Gladys and Bob got married in Bristol. He put down his profession as Trick Motorcycle Rider; Gladys, however, does not give her profession. At some time Gladys, Bob and Curley Lou Cody also appeared at Victoria Park, in Swansea, where yet another local, Taffy Williams, a dirt-track rider, accepted the £50 offer to ride the wall – he must ride for one minute, remain on the blue line at the top of the wall for one minute come down safely and walk out of the wall with assistance. The price for seeing this challenge was raised from 6d to 2 shillings and 4d, quite expensive. There is no report as to whether he succeeded.

By 9 July Speedy Bob Lee and Gladys Soutter were together riding for Wizards on the Wall at Central Pier, Blackpool, where they stayed for the summer season. The flyer in my possession says 'Riding along from success to success as week after week rolls by!' although again they are both advertised as Americans. Performances were every half-hour.

RIDING ALONG FROM SUCCESS TO SUCCESS
AS WEEK AFTER WEEK ROLLS BY!

WIZARDS ON THE WALL

Meets the Public Demand for Thrills ! and more Thrills ! !

Featuring SPEEDY BOB LEE, and DARE-DEVIL GLADYS SOUTTER.

Death-Defying Motor Cyclists

Americans Performing Hair-raising Tricks on a wall as straight as the walls of your own home.

"A SHOW of a TOTALLY DIFFERENT KIND," AT THE

CENTRAL PIER, Blackpool

PERFORMANCES EVERY HALF-HOUR.

"So Good that Interest never Slackens."

—Entire British Press

Gazette, 9th July 1930

Wizards on the Wall – Blackpool flyer 9 July, 1930

Robert Restall and Gladys Soutter

Gladys on wall no hands

By August 1930, Gladys was pregnant. In October 1930, Gladys went to the Munich Oktoberfest to see my mother ride on the wall there.

It is also possible that she was riding on a French wall for a time as Mlle Gladys with M. Jacquot.

Le Mur de la Mort postcard

In April 1931 Gladys and Robert's son was born, so for a while Gladys had to give up riding to look after the baby. However, I believe that my grandparents looked after him for some time.

Meanwhile Robert had been training with the Thanet Motoring Club in Westbrook. He and another member, E. J. Milgate, left to ride in Rosia Hartz in Germany and then continued to tour the Continent with a wall, probably a Wizard on the Wall one, or one of Robert Restall's walls.

The American and Canadian riders had problems with visas for Britain. These visas were very short duration and some riders criss-crossed the Atlantic to renew them. Many other riders took off to ride on the Continent where, presumably, they got longer visas. One rider even wrote to British Immigration to complain that short visas meant they could not fulfil their riding contracts in the UK. In 1932 the UK Board of Trade asked the British rider Jack North to ride for them to decide whether the US riders would be granted extended visas. He rode so well that the visas dried up.[8]

When Robert returned from Germany the couple decided that they would have to find a new riding partner for him, since Gladys had to look after the baby. They did have to pay the bills somehow. By this time Gladys had bought a Wall of Death – the two of them interviewed potential riders and Gladys choose Mildred Shelley, a British girl. Robert and Mildred then went to Hamburg with Gladys's wall and possibly toured other Continental countries. It is virtually impossible to get records or photos from Germany because so much was destroyed in the war, but I do have a photo of Robert and Mildred in a night club.

What then happened was not what Gladys had anticipated. Robert abandoned her and their baby and started living with Mildred. After riding in Germany for some time the couple returned to England. Robert dropped his riding name Speedy Bob Lee and they rode for a while as Robert and Mildred Lee, but advertised themselves as brother and sister! In 1934 they had a baby and in 1937 Robert, Mildred and their baby returned to Canada. In the meantime they had left Gladys's wall in Hamburg and Gladys had to go and bring it back to the UK. This was particularly difficult since Germany was on the brink of war. The wall was brought back and presumably she sold it to someone because it was at Olympia after the war, after which time she had given up riding.

So not only had Robert abandoned her and their child, she also lost her riding partner. She was never to hear from him again. So she started riding with her sister, my mother, which is covered in Chapter 9. Gladys gave up riding some time before the Second World War.

Robert Ernest Restall was killed in the Oak Island Mine Tragedy in 1965. Ironically his son Robert Restall was also killed but it was not Gladys's son – Robert Restall had another son ten years later in Canada whom he also called Robert! However, he never divorced Gladys so it was not until she read about his death in the British newspapers that she obtained his death certificate and as a widow was able at last to marry again. She married Jack Lancaster in 1974 – he had also been a Wall of Death rider in the mid-1930s and they had ridden together in 1932 and 1933 in Scotland.

---

1. Ronnie Power, MBE. Retired theatrical agent.
2. Undated press cutting.
3. Undated press cutting.
4. Undated press cutting.
5. Advertisement *Western Daily Press*, 1 April 1930 (reproduced with kind permission of the British Newspaper Archive, www.britishnewspaperarchive.co.uk).
6. Undated press cutting.
7. *Gloucester Citizen*, 1 April 1930 (reproduced with kind permission of the British Newspaper Archive, www.britishnewspaperarchive.co.uk).
8. Alan Mercer, Wall of Death historian.

Chapter 7

Winifred Mary Doris Soutter, My Mother

Born: 23 January, 1915, at Camberwell, London.
Married: George Todd, 23 May 1935, at Bromley, Kent.
Died: 11 July 1988.
Daughter: Ann Todd, born 9 February 1941, Banwell, Somerset.
Riding names: Fearless Winnie, Dare-Devil Winnie,
Dare-Devil Fearless Winnie, then Winnie Soutter, then Win Todd.
She rode the wall from 1930 until 1952. Owned a wall 1939–1956.

My mother was six years younger than Gladys, her sister.

Richard Lesley Stainfield, my great-uncle, was born in 1905. At the age of 24, Dick lived in Westbrook, Kent, with his mother, who ran a boarding house there. He also owned a shop called Stainfield Motors, selling and repairing motorcycles. He was an agent of Velocette and Arial motorcycles. He was also a star grass-track rider and captain of the Thanet Motor Club.

Dick Stainfield's shop (copyright Stuart Soutter)

Wyn and Robert Restall, January 1930

At the age of 13 or 14 my mother went to live with Dick's mother and her uncle and went to school locally – probably because her parents had so many other children to look after. Unlike Gladys my mother could ride a motorcycle and was a keen member of the Thanet Motor Club. My great-uncle taught her to ride a Rex Acme bike on a grass track, on which she was proficient by the age of 14. She stated she 'acquired my craze for motorcycles' and also acted as a pit mechanic for her 'youthful' uncle.[1]

So when Robert Restall met Gladys and persuaded her to learn to ride, my aunt told my mother, who was then fourteen. My mother went to London late in 1929 to meet Robert, then Robert and Gladys went to Westbrook very early in 1930. My mother had a photo of herself and Robert and a note which states that he taught her to ride the wall.

However, the Wall of Death rider Johnnie Parr, who rode with my mother in October 1930, wrote to *The World's Fair* saying that my mother had told him that the Restall brothers were not very experienced riders and could only do straight rides and it was my mother who taught herself to perform the various tricks and taught the brothers to trick ride. In a very long letter he pointed out at the end:

> ... has he heard of the 16 year old girl rider who does all the motorcycle tricks which were done by the American riders and who, although taught to ride straight by an American [Canadian actually] learned all the tricks herself. [2]

On 20 May 1930, Robert's two brothers arrived in the UK from York, Ontario, Canada:[3] William Arthur Restall, born 1913 in Ontario, was already a Wall of Death rider (in Europe his riding name was Billy Lee or

Wild Billie Lee); and Goldwin Charles Restall, born 1910 in Ontario, also a rider. In Europe his riding name was Curley Lee or Goldy Lee. They then went to Westbrook and joined the Thanet Motor Club and both stayed in Dick's mother's boarding house. They gave their address as care of 42 Sussex Place, South Kensington – the Morgan Hastings offices. By the time they arrived Robert had already married Gladys.

In 1999 I received a letter from a Fred Rothwell, who was a member of the Thanet Motor Club in 1929/1930.[4] He stated that in 1930 a number of members of the club built a Wall of Death on a piece of ground next to a pub on the Ramsgate Road. Peter Josling was a member of the club whose father ran a building company and it was he who instigated the project and probably drew up plans for building a wall. Rothwell himself helped build the wall as did my great-uncle Dick. Rothwell clearly remembered my mother and sent me photos of her at the dirt-track meetings. However, these British dirt-track riders could not have built a wall without the help of the three Restall brothers.

In January 1999 the *Daily Telegraph* ran an article on the Wall of Death and Rothwell wrote to the motoring correspondent telling him about this wall being built in 1930. He also stated that the wall went on tour and whilst in Berlin, Adolf Hitler witnessed a performance and made a special presentation to the riders to commemorate his visit. This could have been in 1931, when Goldy Restall rode the wall in Berlin.[5]

By very early in 1930 my mother had quickly learned to ride the wall and had adopted her riding name, 'Fearless Winnie'. She worked for Morgan Hastings on a Wizards on the Wall and was teamed up with an American, Louis C. Shwarootz.

Shwarootz, born in 1909, had arrived in the UK on 6 September 1929, aged 20.[6] His riding names were either Curly Lou Cody, Curly Cody, Curly Lew Cody, Lou Cody, Speedy Curly Lee, Suicide Cody or Suicide Curley Lou Cody. He should not be confused with his brother Cyclone Jack Cody who arrived at about the same time. When he arrived in September 1929 Curly Lou Cody did not ride for at least six weeks – he had had an accident in America and broken a collar bone. Eventually he was interviewed in Peterborough and asked whether he and Suicide Jockey Roland, with whom he had arrived in England, were doing well. His reply was that 'in London they had 20,000 people a week but some of the other towns were poor'. They were then going south, keeping on the move from town to town until the coming of the summer season again, 'when we shall settle at a seaside resort'.[7]

In February 1930 he was riding with Suicide Jockey Roland at Cheltenham but in March he was riding with Speedy Bob Lee, all of whom worked for Morgan Hastings. In June 1930, he was riding on a

Wizards on the Wall at Newport. Over a thousand people wanted to see the act, so many in fact that both entry staircases collapsed – the police and ambulances had to attend but fortunately the crowd that had been thrown to the ground were not seriously injured. Although the staircases had been tested for weight they had not been tested for a crush of people trying to get up the stairs.

At about the same time my mother rode as Dare-Devil Winnie in Weston-super-Mare with Reckless Rudy Coombs and Speedy Curly Lee (Goldwin Charles Restall).[8]

Early in 1930 on New Brighton promenade it was announced that Curly Lew Cody had just arrived and 'rides his machine BLINDFOLDED on Wizards on the Wall'.[9]

Photographs appeared in the local newspaper with the caption 'A Cyclonic Storm of Thrills and Hair-Raising Stunts by Suicide Curley Cody of the Wizards of the Wall New Brighton'. His riding partner was my mother, Dare-Devil Fearless Winnie (although she was referred to as American).

A Cyclonic Storm – Suicide Cody top of wall, 1930

NEW BRIGHTON'S LATEST ATTRACTION.
A SHOW OF OUTSTANDING IMPORTANCE.

WIZARDS on the WALL

Amazing! Startling! Thrilling!

Featuring

Suicide Cody and Fearless Winnie.

Death Defying Motor Cyclists.

You have seen Dirt Track and Speedway Racing, but see this Super Thrill of America's best Dare-devil Riders at top Speed in sheer defiance of the laws of gravity—around a wall as straight as the walls in your own home

AT FROM 60 TO 100 MILES PER HOUR.

HAIR RAISING TRICKS

At this speed shown to 30,000 persons weekly.

Seen by the Prince of Wales, Mr. Ramsay MacDonald, Sir Henry Segrave, Capt. Malcolm Campbell, Kaye Don, and other famous men.
All were AMAZED.

Read what the Papers say—

"It is the biggest thrill of all."—"Daily Mail."

"A difficult and dangerous-looking feat."—"Daily Mirror."

"An astonishing exhibition of nerve and dare-devilry."—"Daily Express."

"Skill and nerve required to ride the 'Wall' is possessed by very few humans."—"Pearson's Weekly."

"Everyone who enjoys watching daring feats should not miss to see this performance."—"Daily Sketch."

Etc. Etc.

Special Engagement for Summer Season
Continuous Performance Daily from 10 a.m. to 11 p.m.

Palace Grounds (opposite Battery),
PROMENADE, New Brighton.

1930 New Brighton flyer – Wizards on the Wall

An original 1930 flyer in my possession states the New Brighton wall was a special engagement for the summer season and the show ran from 10 a.m. to 11 p.m. (a very long time to ride in one day). Some time during that season the show was visited by none other than the Prince of Wales, Mr Ramsay MacDonald, Sir Henry Seagrave, Capt. Malcolm Campbell and Kay Don, all of whom were amazed. Naishtad quickly put this onto the flyers and posters also saying that 30,000 people a week were visiting the show, and that the riders were performing hair-raising tricks at 60–100 miles an hour. Naishtad was also quoted on all the national papers; for instance the *Daily Express* said 'An astonishing exhibition of nerve and dare-devilry'.

In September 1930 *The Motorcycle Magazine* printed an article entitled 'Living on Risks! A "Wall of Death" Rider Describes this Sensational Act'. Having first described a wall he continued:

> My 'barker' having attracted an audience, myself and lady partner start our act, our motors having been filled up and got ready for us.
>
> It is a popular idea that we have to work up a high speed around the banking at the bottom of the wall before we go up: this is wrong, since it is possible for a good rider to put his motor up on the wall at the first circuit.
>
> Our act starts with the lady going up first, then me, and then both together. While riding I perform a number of variations, such as letting go of the handlebars, standing on the rests, sitting on one side of the machine, etc., etc., and generally doing stuff that (although I say it) you would not care to try on the road unless you had practised for a very long time.
>
> The thing that is most likely to lead to a crack-up is a tyre going, or else the motor locking up. We also have to stand the risk of the audience dropping cigarette ash into our eyes, and temporarily blinding us.[10]

He finally commented saying in the States a lion was introduced into an act – but this attraction was not allowed in England. This was clearly not the case since by September 1930, several riders in the UK had lions in their act and it goes to prove that newspaper reports cannot always be believed. I think this article was by Cody and his partner was my mother.

Cody clearly had an accident at some time but was riding the next day. Between the two of them they had coined the phrase 'a frown is always out of style, a Wizard always wears a smile', which my mother noted in her photograph album.

Photo *Last night's crash,* Suicide Cody

In New Brighton Sam Naishtad, their manager, decided to take a pillion ride. The long press cutting in my collection describes how Sam went on Suicide Cody's bike – no doubt my mother was watching with great interest.

> Suicide Cody briefly instructed me to keep still, lean right or left as he directed and not to grip the handlebars too tightly. A preliminary wobble as we were pushed off, and the motor snarled into life with first a sputtering cough, then rising to crescendo roar as Cody took a fist-full of twist grip. We hit the sharp angle of the narrow starting track with a bump, thudded round smoothly enough for two laps, and then, just as I was beginning to think what an easy and over-rated pastime this was, the machine seemed to gather itself together and with a snarl of rage, as though trying to escape from the narrow confines of the thirty foot drum, hurled itself at the perpendicular wall. EVERYTHING TURNS BLACK. The memory of that first ten second lingers vividly. Still low down on the wall, below the half-way line, we romped round. I turned giddy, more giddy than I ever thought it possible to be without passing away. Everything turned black before my eyes and I had a curious impression that I was dead and had been stood on my head! Then I came back to life again, realised I wasn't dead and wished I were. But still that appalling giddiness. … I could hear the roar of the engine; I could feel the cold night air cutting into me, and I was aware of the dull rumbling of the broad hard tyres on the wooden wall, but still I could not see. Then another sensation overcame the giddiness. I realised that I was paralysed. My body was jammed solidly against the tank, my feet immovable on the rests and my hands gripping the bars in the middle in front of me. I couldn't move my head even. Gradually, as though a powerful hand had gripped my neck, I was forced down over the bars. OUT OF CONTROL. I heard Cody shout, and realised that I was gripping the bars with super-human strength and that for the moment we were out of control. I had enough sense left to release my grip and, then, from somewhere came a whistle. I felt the speed decrease, heard the engine slow down, caught the spitting crack of a blow-back as the cut-out came into operation, and then, still high on the wall, I began to see. I saw the boards racing under the front wheel, caught a glimpse of the red line and as we dropped down in spirals towards the floor, saw a glimpse of yellow and green, the colours of an advertisement for a popular brand of petrol and oil, on the floor below …

> The after effects of that ride were curious. I was only conscious for the first few minutes of an extraordinary light-headedness. My arms felt like feathers and every movement I made seemed ridiculously effortless. I had been on the wall barely a minute. I look back on that minute as the most crowded in my life. ... I am inclined to believe that Dare-Devil Winnie Soutter and Lou Cody have looked so long into the eyes of death that they have stared him out of countenance.[11]

Also during that season he wrote another long article, briefly explaining the wall's development in America, saying that it took 12–18 months to learn to ride the wall (clearly not correct) and they first had to learn to overcome giddiness, temporary blindness and the terrific pressure of centrifugal force. He also stated that, contrary to advertisements, the maximum speed was round about 60 or 65 miles per hour – above that is suicidal – and the lowest speed about 35 mph. The machines used were stripped Indian Scouts and riders could only use their own machines, so sensitive were they to the touch and feel of their mounts. 'Visitors will see a robust maiden, of 15 years of age – Dare-Devil Winnie Soutter, the youngest rider in the UK' (which at that time was certainly true).[12]

Before the New Brighton season in 1930 Speedy Curly Lee, Dare-Devil Winnie and Reckless Rudy Coombs also appeared at the Old Pier, Weston-super-Mare. The flyer announces 'Records Broken! Two Millions Thrilled! All England Talking! – Wizards on the Wall – an American Trio' (wrong again). Performances were every half-hour.[13]

By this time Naishtad was stepping up the publicity. Commercially produced postcards of the riders with their names were sold at the walls, according to my uncle Jack Soutter, for 2d each. Fearless Winnie and Suicide Cody also featured on a cartoon novelty card drawn by Edward Stuart which said 'stick pin in centre and spin'.

Cartoon, Fearless Winnie and Suicide Cody

By the time they rode at New Brighton their names were painted on the tanks of their bikes, Fearless Wyn and Curley Cody, and they each wore riding tops with their names, Wyn and Curly, embroidered on. There were commercial photos of Gladys, Robert Restall, Wyn and Curley Lou Cody, which were sold as souvenirs.

Fearless Wyn on named bike

Wyn Soutter and Suicide Cody on bally of wall

Suicide Cody on named bike

Their act resulted in considerable press coverage not only in local but also national papers. What was always mentioned was the very young age of my mother, who was displaying the most considerable skill and nerve whilst performing her numerous tricks on the wall. The fact that so many famous people had been to see the act was also commented on in various press reports. For my mother, just out of school, meeting all these famous people must have been quite an exciting experience. After appearing there for the whole summer season my mother and Curley had an even greater adventure – see Chapter 8.

---

1. Wyn Todd, personal recorded memories.
2. 'Wall Riding Feats', *The World's Fair*, 5 November 1932.
3. Ancestry.co.uk.
4. Letter from Fred Rothwell to the author, 1999.
5. Letter from Fred Rothwell to Phillip Sampson, *Daily Telegraph* motoring correspondent, 4 January 1999.
6. Ancestry.co.uk.
7. Undated press cutting.
8. The *Weston-super-Mare Gazette*, undated.
9. Undated press cutting.
10. *The Motorcycle Magazine*, September 1930.
11. Undated press cutting 'A Ride on the Wall of Death with a Wizard' by Sam Naishtad.
12. Undated press cutting.
13. Weston-Super-Mare undated flyer.

Chapter 8

Munich Oktoberfest, 1930

My mother had clearly impressed Naishtad and the Wizards on the Wall owners because in 1930 she was contracted to ride the wall along with Curley Lou Cody at the Munich Oktoberfest in Germany which opened on 19 October.

The Oktoberfest was an enormous annual fair in Munich which had started in 1810 to celebrate the marriage of Crown Prince Ludwig, later King Ludwig, and Princess Theresa von Sachsen-Hildburghausen but was intended for the Bavarian population. It has run almost annually ever since, with the exception of twenty-four years, which were cancelled because of wars, other political events or cholera epidemics. It is still held every year.

By 1930 the site in the centre of Munich city had become enormous. There were two walls, the first that of Capt. Bob and Jenny Perry and a second wall called the *Amerikan Steilwand – Todesfahrer* (America Wall of Death – Death Riders), the wall my mother rode, the frontage and bally of which were far larger than the Perry wall. Although walls had been seen in Germany before, it was the first time they had appeared at the famous Oktoberfest.

Postcard – Munich Oktoberfest wall from afar

Bally of wall with Fearless Winnie and other riders

In October 1930 my mother went to ride there, chaperoned by my grandmother, presumably because she was only fifteen, or perhaps because my mother did not have a passport. They stayed at the Hotel Wolff and had to report to the police station every day; an unsubstantiated family rumour is that the Germans thought my grandmother was a spy and their hotel room was frequently searched.

According to my mother she rode for seventeen days from 11 a.m. until past midnight to packed houses and they had a terrific reception. Naishtad had negotiated with two famous German Riding Masters, called Gabriel and Ruprecht, who had been involved in the Oktoberfest for many years. The four riders on the wall, their names painted above the bally, were Fearless Winnie, Curley Lou Cody, Crasher Evans and Speedy Jo Parr. The bally was enormous and clearly used for publicity. One photo has ten people on it: three riders on bikes, including my mother, a man in a top hat, a man with a megaphone and two other men dressed in suits. I suspect one of the men in suits was Naishtad. Naishtad had a special poster and a postcard printed and distributed. It featured a man and a woman riding together on one motorbike – this was my mother and Curley Lou Cody. The audience is shown looking down from the walkround. A larger poster has Gabriel and Ruprecht and Oktoberfest 1930 printed on it.

Naishtad's postcard to my mother

The flyers and the postcard printed by Naishtad are slightly different and do not include Gabriel and Ruprecht's names. The postcards were for sale to the public no doubt. An original postcard in my collection is signed 'to Fearless Winnie from Sam Naishtad'.

The original flyer in German in my collections says:

> You and the whole of Germany can see the incredible feats of the dare-devil motorcyclists in the ride of death on the American Wall of Death! For the first time in Germany.
>
> The speed-loving Curly Lou Cody and Winnie Soutter ride on the totally perpendicular wall, 7 metres high and 11 metres in diameter, and at a speed of around 150 kmph perform the most incredible acrobatics on their racing bikes. The bikes they ride are 1000 cc 'Indian' type. [Although they were actually 600 cc.] On the Johannesplatz for the October Festival.
>
> Breath-taking! Sensational! Thrilling!
>
> Never in your life have you seen anything like it. The world's press is talking about it.[1]

Flyer in German

However, as has been pointed out before, in the UK showmen with rights to a showground often arranged for walls to be present. For the

Oktoberfest this was not the case. The wall which presented the most daring and spectacular show was chosen.

This wall belonged to the Wizards on the Wall company not Gabriel and Ruprecht and it was not an American wall. It must have been a logistical nightmare for Naishtad – not only did he have to have the wall, bikes, spares and lorries transported across the channel and driven into Germany. He also had four riders, plus no doubt a spare one or two in case of serious accident, my grandmother, a spieler, lorry drivers, himself and any staff to put the wall up and take it down.

My mother's German press cuttings indicate the number of newspapers which reported on the wall. Because the wall was called Amerikan many reports wrongly stated all the riders were American and several did not name the riders. However, one unnamed newspaper stated that the American Wall was the greatest sensation of the Oktoberfest and named the riders:

> Curley Lou Cody, Winnie Soutter – a charming blonde girl not yet 16 – and Johnnie Parr were the names of the three young Americans [wrong nationalities of course] who in a wooden cauldron 7 metres high and 12 metres diameter execute their tricks on their Harley-Davidson Motorcycles.

This is also wrong. The riders rode Indian Scouts. Another illustrated newspaper article shows nine different photos of what to see at the fair and Curly Cody riding his bike on the wall is one of them, with the caption 'The breath-taking acrobatic feats on Carl Gabriel's Wall of Death'.[2]

Another said:

> Racing in the pit of hell. Who wants to have a go? The manager asked the audience this question, but his only answer is vigorous shakes of the head. Nobody wants to challenge the American Wall of Death riders who are among the biggest sensations at the October Festival. Curley Lou Cody, Winnie Soutter – a charming blonde girl, just 16 years of age [she was only 15] – and Johnnie Parr are the names of the three daring young Americans who perform the craziest stunts on their Harley-Davidson motorbikes in a wooden drum 7 metres high and 12 metres in diameter. One minute they are pursuing one another round the perpendicular wall at breakneck speed, next they are riding with no hands, then they are sitting on the handlebars. The audience looks down into the pit from the stand, their hair stands on end, and the tension takes their breath away. They heave a sigh of

> relief when the Wall of Death riders are once again safe on the floor of the giant drum, and express both their thanks for the performance and their pleasure at the successful end of the life-endangering stunts. This venture is presented by Carl Gabriel together with Ruprecht – we are accustomed to getting only the best from Gabriel. The Wall of Death riders always have a full house, for word has already spread about the tremendous feats performed by the three Americans.[3]

However, I suspect that Harley-Davidson tried to get in on the act because there is a notice on the front of the wall advertising them.

I think for my mother her visit to the Oktoberfest must have been an unbelievably wonderful experience. Despite the long hours she rode she did have time to do other things, and probably stayed longer after the Oktoberfest had finished. Since my grandmother had never been abroad it was probably an experience for her too. She had photos, mostly including other riders, visiting the zoo, riding bicycles in the countryside and watching or perhaps participating in grass-track riding in the countryside. She would also have seen a variety of things at the Oktoberfest itself – the very large opening ceremony parade, which would have included horse-drawn drays with barrels of beer, brass bands, shooting teams, people in German national costume, all manner of entertainments. Once it opened she would no doubt have visited all the enormous beer halls, in which German food was eaten and you could also get coffee – not sure if my mother drank alcohol at that age! These huge beer halls were, and still are to this day, one of the great attractions. She had a photo of Gladys and Curly outside Carl Gabriel's Hippodrome with a note that says 'outside the famous Oktoberfest Hippodrome where showmen from all over the world meet to eat and drink'.

Inside the Hippodrome was a circular sand ring, in which you could see twenty-five horse riders whilst you were drinking. The horse riders were the public! And quite often drunk! Amongst the hundreds of amusements on offer was the ice palace, a wax bust of a German mass-murderer and all the usual fairground rides, including ones she had never seen before: carousels, dodgems, shooting ranges, helter skelters, German craft stalls, souvenir stalls, etc. I have no doubt she also visited the other wall, since she was friendly with Jenny Perry.

Another rider she clearly met was Kitty Muller (1910–1990) from Munich, who was twenty. In 1929 Kitty had visited the UK and the family of a showman. That is where she first saw a Wall of Death and decided that was what she wanted to do. By 1930 she was riding a wall in Hamburg and is thought to be the first-ever female German rider. Clearly Kitty, who was already smitten, went to the Oktoberfest and watched my mother and the others riding. Later Kitty rode with Johnnie Parr in Sweden. Kitty and my mother were friends for the rest of their lives.

Gladys Soutter and Suicide Curly outside the Oktoberfest Hippodrome

---

1. Undated German press cutting.
2. Undated German press cutting.
3. Undated German press cutting.

Chapter 9

The Soutter Sisters Ride Together – 1931–1933

Robert Restall's two brothers had arrived in the UK in May 1930. My mother told me that he had formed a company and had three walls built in Germany.

After Munich and early in 1931 my mother was back in Westgate with the Thanet Motor Club and her uncle, Dick Stainfield. The club had, the previous year, built a Wall of Death and in an undated local paper report clearly written in the spring of 1931 the following details appeared:

> During the next few days several members of the Thanet Motoring Club will leave the town to fulfil engagements as Wall of Death Riders. They are R. Restall, G. Restall, W. Restall, E. J. Milgate, Miss R. James and Miss W. Soutter.
>
> G. and R. Restall and Milgate are to spend a short period in Rosla Hartz, Germany. Milgate and R. Restall to tour the Continent, and G. Restall to fulfil a season's engagement in Berlin.
>
> Miss James and W. Restall will appear in Hamburg and Budapest.
>
> Miss W. Soutter will take her sister Miss G. Soutter and a girl pillion rider to Scarborough. The Restall brothers, who are Canadians, have ridden on the Death Wall in England, America and on the Continent. Whilst Miss W. Soutter, who is a Margate girl, was billed at Scarborough throughout last summer.
>
> During the past few months the Thanet Motoring Club has built a Death Wall.'[1]

So it would appear that the three Restall brothers toured the three walls that Robert had had built in Germany. What exactly did touring the Continent entail? It is virtually impossible to get information about the Wall of Death on the Continent in the years 1930–31, so much was destroyed in the war. However, in 1991 the granddaughter of Miss James sent me a copy of her grandmother's passport for those years. Mary Rachel James (known as Ray) was born in Port Talbot in 1910. In order to travel with the wall she got issued with her passport in April 1931. It was valid for the British Empire, France, Belgium, Luxembourg, Switzerland, Italy, Holland, Spain, Portugal, Germany, Austria, Hungary and the USA. Where she went and when are a bit difficult to decipher because border control stamps in a foreign language are often stamped on top of a previous entry but it would seem that in 1931 and 1932 she was in Hamburg, Munich (where she cashed money in a bank!), Boulogne (where she was not allowed to earn money in France), Budapest (several times), Warsaw, Romania (for one month), Petrovice, Belepett and Poland, staying at Hotel Britannia. She was accompanied by William Restall, whom she called Billy, and I have several photographs of the two of them together.

Ray James' granddaughter has recently found the following reference to their appearance in Budapest:

> She has more fear from the motorbike than the devil. The brave bikers of the English Park's 'Trap of Death', who repeat their neck-breaking performances every day, have rapidly become the most popular attraction. Two young English boys [actually one Canadian] and a Welsh girl – even the oldest is less than 20 years old – have travelled around the world, conquering everybody who has seen them with their amazing tricks. The Prima Donna – Ms. James Rachel Mary [sic], a beautiful blonde lady – is laughing while she talks about her childhood, and says that she has more fear from the motorbike than the devil. Now she is the world-famous queen of the motorbike. Her two partners – Edwin James Millgate, almost 20 years old, and William (Bill) Restall, just 17 – started their careers as racers. These determined brave boys were found by a manager, with whom they signed a big-money contact. And so they became artistes. In the English Park every night, while the Trap of Death's travellers are working, a pale-faced person is jittering – their manager. Only the public's noisy clapping comforts him: 'Thank God, nothing bad happened today.'[2]

In December 1932 Ray James travelled to New York, with a three-month visa, in the company of William and Goldwin Restall. She returned to the UK but I don't think the two brothers returned to Europe, their father had been taken ill.

Robert Restall meanwhile, whilst riding in Riechenbach in Germany, broke an arm and had a commercial photograph taken (to sell) with his arm in a sling on the bally of the wall. There is a car on the bally too so perhaps Millgate drove a car on the wall. They had built two small cars for the wall in Ramsgate.

Robert Restall, accident, Germany, 1930s

Meanwhile Gladys had given birth to her son and with her husband touring Europe she had to find another riding partner. Morgan Hastings asked my mother to put on a show at Scarborough and choose two other girls to ride. Aged only 16, that must have been quite a responsibility for my mother, still the youngest rider in the UK. She had two staff to look after, both older than her. She also had to maintain the bikes and the wall and cope with the numerous press requests and photographs. Naishtad does not appear to have been present in Scarborough.

So my mother, her sister and Josie Conquest started riding together for Wizards on the Wall. They spent the summer season at Scarborough and my collection of original press cuttings suggests they were very popular.

YOU MUST SEE THE SHOW OF SHOWS!
The fulfilment of your most extravagant dreams of entertainment!
Featuring THREE ENGLISH GIRL RIDERS, Fearless WINNIE, Dare-Devil GLADYS, and Reckless JOSIE.

WIZARDS ON THE WALL

DEATH-DEFYING MOTOR CYCLISTS

An English Trio presenting the only show of its kind in the world, consisting of Hair-raising Tricks and Dare-devil Riding on a Wall as straight as the walls of your own home.

THRILLS! THRILLS! NERVE-TINGLING THRILLS!

CENTRE SOUTH FORESHORE

PERFORMANCES EVERY HALF-HOUR.
The LARGEST SENSATIONAL THRILLER in the Outdoor Amusement World.

Wizards on the Wall advertisement, Scarborough

An advertisement announced 'The fulfilment of your most extravagant dreams of entertainment! ... Wizards on the Wall – death-defying motorcyclists. Thrills: Thrills: Nerve-tingling thrills! ... the LARGEST SENSATIONAL THRILLER in Outdoor Amusement World', and named the three girls.

There was also an article saying:

> Though only sixteen Winnie Soutter is the Captain of a team of girl trick cyclists, who are daily amazing crowds on the South Shore with hair-raising tricks around a vertical wooden wall, presenting the only show of its kind in the world.

Fearless Winnie on bike, 1931

Performances were every half-hour and they were open thirteen hours a day. My mother also reported:

> We wanted to show that girls have as much nerve as men at the game. ... Gladys and I met Josie Conquest for the first time a few weeks ago and ... we finished our training a week ago.[3]

The *Daily Sketch* printed a picture of the three of them, surrounded by dozens of people, as they set off to give a demonstration on Scarborough sands, although I suspect Gladys was riding pillion.[4]

There was also a write-up reporting they 'spend 13 hours a day doing their tricks on ordinary motorcycles with a coolness and a nerve that are amazing'. The *Sunday Chronicle* also had an article entitled 'Out to beat men at daring', 'performing stunts that men are afraid to do. Yet a few months ago Winnie was going to school, her sister was a film actress and their partner was on the stage.'

Scarborough wall front

My mother had her second wall accident in July in Scarborough. When she reached the bottom the audience applauded because they thought it was part of the act. The whole episode was reported in *The World's Fair*, calling it an 'unrehearsed thrill at Scarborough'.

> The large audience who were witnessing the performance of Fearless Winnie Soutter at the Death Drome on the Foreshore at Scarborough were provided with an unrehearsed thrill on Thursday July 16 and the wall rider herself had a miraculous escape. After performing various stunts the rider was preparing for her final trick, when for some unknown reasons the machine picked up speed, causing her to lose her balance. The machine made five circuits round the drome with Fearless Winnie lying with her head and shoulders rubbing on the back wheel. Mr. Jack Harlow the manager ... immediately realized her predicament and attempted to grasp her as she came round the wall. At the third attempt he managed to spring up the wall and grasped the rider's arm, jerking her from the machine to the well of the drome. The machine then made two circuits of the wall riderless, struck the safely cable and crashed to the bottom, exactly on the spot where but a few seconds before Winnie had lain. Fearless Winnie who was conscious all the time did not lose her nerve. Although only 17 [she was 16] and one of the youngest riders in the country she certainly upheld her name of 'Fearless'. The audience, under the impression that it was part of the show, applauded vigorously.[5]

My mother could not ride for 2–3 weeks. Early in 1932 Morgan Hastings started selling their walls and no longer employed my mother and aunt. A possible reason could have been that the visas for the American and Canadian riders were not being renewed, so there were few male riders.

In January 1932, my mother put an advertisement in *The World's Fair*: 'Fearless Winnie Soutter, Drome Rider – open for engagement early this year as a straight or trick rider. 2 years' experience. 9 Seymour Terrace, Anerley, London SE20 [my grandparents' home].'[6] Considering how famous she had become this advertisement was somewhat modest. However, it was seen by Codona and within a week my mother was riding on Codona's wall in Scotland, along with Gladys. The Codonas were a large family in Scotland, most of whom were involved in fairs and amusement parks, which they are still running today.

My mother and aunt appeared in Edinburgh during the first weeks of 1932 at the amusement park owned by Frank and William Codona. The show was called the Death Riders. The front of the wall had a large poster proclaiming: 'Out to beat the men. The New Death Riders. A troupe of Britain's foremost Lady Motor Cyclists, Daring Gladys Soutter and Fearless Winnie Soutter.' There are three riders on the bally, one a man called Jack Lancaster, and a barker with a bowler hat. Codona had been presenting Death Riders since 1931 in Scotland, when a wall was present at the Links Market, Kirkcaldy, and Jack Lancaster rode for him.

My mother and aunt became members of the Kirkcaldy Motor Club and clearly managed to see a good part of the local scenery – my mother had a friend in the club who was a photographer and there are a lot of photos of the friends all on motorbikes touring the lakes etc. My mother became friendly with J. K. Swanston, who later went on to win the Isle of Man Grand Prix several times and died recently aged 104. Sand Racing was very popular with motorcyclists at the time and my mother attended those races with other club members and probably also rode in them. Captain Eric (Winkle) Brown, Royal Navy, Britain's greatest war pilot, was also local and could well have been a club member and he rode a Wall of Death for a short time locally.

The New Death Riders – Scotland, 1932

My mother's photographs show that they appeared, amongst other places, in Braemar, Aberdeen, Perth, Forres, Nairn, Broughty Ferry and Aikey Brae but don't indicate which dates. An article, written in 1970, records one Scottish person's memories of Aikey Brae:

> ... so you took her to see the Death Riders on the Wall of Death, clinging to their motor bikes like flies in a jar,

> screaming up nearly to the rim of the giant barrel when they were at full speed, their tyres nearly touching your toes where you stared down at them from the railing. Three motor bikes were on the wall at one time, with a game bit quine [girl] on the pillion of one of them, flying round and round like a bool in a brose caup, the roar of their engines like to deafen you and the speed of their machines shaking the wooden structure under your feet, while all the time you were feart that they flew over the top of the wall. But eventually, when they felt you'd had you money's worth they snorted down their bikes and descended to the grass circle, when everybody threw down their pennies to the riders, because it was said that no insurance would take them on at such a risk. This was above your admission money, and maybe it was a gimmick, but you felt it was worth it and you threw your meck with the others, maybe a tanner if you felt big-hearted. So you came down the steps from the tower of death and went and had a keek at one of Cleopatra's handmaidens ....'[7]

At Broughty Carnival in July 1932, it was reported that 'two beautiful belles will provide an added attraction to the Death Riders stunts'.

The wall often led younger members of the public to try to copy riders, as illustrated by the following:

> Cycling Feats at Broughty – A new and thrilling sport, the result maybe, of the visit of the Death Riders in the carnival of last summer, has caught the imagination of the more daring amongst the young blood of Broughty Ferry. The idea is to cycle along the sloping wall between Church Street and Ferry Bay, and this is done without much regard for either the bicycle or the wall, for the wall is broken here and there by flights of steps. The real thrill, discounting the danger of falling on the shingle, is evidently obtained by using the slope to give momentum in the manner of a scenic railway and to dispense with much pedalling.[8]

Fife Free Press & Kirkcaldy Guardian, on 29 April 1933, printed a cartoon of the Links Market attractions which include a Wall of Death with the quote: 'Hell Drivers say Hello! We gave up motoring when we saw the Death Riders.'

On 25 August for one week Codona's Wall of Death Sensation was advertised in the local paper to be seen at Riverside, in Wick. It featured: 'Fearless Miss Winnie Soutter, the 18 year old girl who has outclassed the men with her death-defying acrobatic stunts together with her partner Easy Jack [Jack Lancaster].'

Cartoon: Links Market, 1933

In Scotland in June 1932 my mother had her third accident, hurting her knee-cap and unable to ride for a month, but she never had another accident after that. This was probably on the New Esplanade in Dundee. A friend from the Kirkcaldy Motor Club sent her this poem:

A certain young lady of London
Rode her bike with such careless abandon
That she came off the wall
The result of the fall
Was she's only one leg left to stand on.

This certain young lady I note,
Has pretensions of being a poet
She made up a rhyme
'Bout me starting in time
As my bicycle never could mote.

The letter was also sent in a somewhat decorative envelope. My mother also recorded in photographs the damage to her bike as a result of the fall.

Envelope sent to my mother

They spent the 1933 summer season at a Scottish resort with Codona's wall. Near this seaside resort, on a different fairground, my father, George Todd, and one of his brothers, Bob, were riding for another Wall of Death, so that is where my mother met my father and my uncle for the first time.

---

1. Undated press report.
2. Budapest magazine, Summer 1931, translation.
3. *Sunday Chronicle*, 31 May 1931 (reproduced with kind permission of the British Newspaper Archive, www.britishnewspaperarchive.co.uk).
4. *Daily Sketch*, 27 May 1931.
5. *The World's Fair*, 25 July 1931.
6. Ibid., 9 January 1932.
7. With thanks to Aberdeenshire Local Studies.
8. *The Evening Telegraph*, 17 May 1932 (reproduced with kind permission of the British Newspaper Archive, www.britishnewspaperarchive.co.uk).

Chapter 10
Jack Lancaster, My Uncle by Marriage

Born: 1900. Married: Gladys Soutter in 1974. Died: 1992.
No children.
Riding name: Easy Jack, from early 1930 to after the war, briefly.

Unlike most riders, Uncle Jack was educated at a private school, and he was also a magician. I have very little information about this Uncle Jack's (I had three!) riding career except for him riding in Scotland with Codona's Wall in the 1930s. In 1930 the Codona Brothers had several adverts in *The World's Fair* asking for a 'ride of death' with a rider as well as a Globe of Death.

In December that year their wall appeared at Abbeyhill, I assume with Uncle Jack riding. By April 1931 it was reported about Easy Jack that 'his riding is the main topic of conversation throughout the district and his name has become a household name'.[1]

Later in April he appeared at the Links Market where it was reported:

> Lancaster is not content merely to take his hands off the handlebars and wave to the spectators but takes Mabel Owen (a local girl) on the handlebars of his machine whilst he is blindfolded with a handkerchief.[2]

Al Evans' wall also appeared at the same time at the Links Market, so competition was fierce. Codona's wall appeared, amongst other places, at Bellahouston, Broughty Carnival, Abbeyhill and Dundee.

In 1932, as stated in the previous chapter, he started riding with my mother and my aunt when Codona's wall travelled all over Scotland in

1932 and 1933 and was called the Death Riders. At the Kirkcaldy Links Market in 1933 Jack had an accident on the wall, by this time called the Drome of Death.

Jack Lancaster front right standing

The Wall of Death made its first appearance in the early 1930s, with its bowl-shaped wooden structure round which motorcyclists hurtled with split second timing watched by the audience from the top. Stuntmen with names like Easy Jack Lancaster, Speedy Sedgwick, Fearless Violet and Cyclone Hogan kept the crowds on the edge of their seats as they carried out their well-rehearsed tricks. Lancaster would take both hands off his machine to wave to the crowds, and then take his female partner on to the handlebars of his bike – blindfold. Small wonder then that he came to grief when his tyre burst during his act; but despite a stitched chin, bandages and a bad limp, he returned to his act next day, with a placard from the *Dundee Courier* announcing his accident hanging at the entrance to the show.

'The crowds used to love the Wall of Death,' said one local man. 'The motorbikes would start on ground level and the crowd would go in and sit on the top of this circular wooden

> shell in circles of tiered seats. The motorbikes kept going round and round and up and up – you had a head like three at the end of it, because the fumes of the exhausts which got trapped inside.'[3]

Uncle Jack was still riding in 1939, when it was reported: 'Jack Lancaster is making his first appearance in this part of the country [England] as he has travelled Scotland for a number of years with a Wall of Death and has been riding with some measure of success.' Whether he owned a wall by then I do not know. Also, after the war he did advertise for work. After Robert Restall had abandoned my aunt, she and Jack lived together for years, finally marrying after Restall's death in Canada, thirty-four years later. We frequently visited them in their later years.

---

1. *The World's Fair*, 4 April 1931.
2. *Fife Free Press & Kirkcaldy Guardian*, 18 April 1931 (reproduced with kind permission of the British Newspaper Archive, www.britishnewspaperarchive.co.uk).
3. Carol McNeill, *Kirkcaldy Links Market*. Fife Council Central Area Libraries and Museums, 2004

Chapter 11
George Todd, My Father

Born: Birmingham, 1910. Married: Winifred Soutter, 23 May 1935.
Died: 1990.

Daughter: Ann Todd, born 1941.

Riding name: only ever rode as George Todd.

Rode 1929–1956. Owned own wall 1932 and then 1939–1956.

My father was one of seven children, having three brothers and three sisters. By 1911 my grandfather was an auctioneer in Birmingham, employing two people, and he was rich enough to employ a servant. He and my grandmother moved around the country ending up in later life living in various places in Kent, renting properties as antique shops, and my grandfather also dabbled in show-business stalls. At one stage he had forty-two shops. Because they moved around a lot my father did not have a very good education. After the Second World War my grandparents rented a large property in Tenterden, Kent, which they ran as an antique shop, and they stayed there for the rest of their lives.

At the age of about 14, in Herne Bay, my father was a delivery boy for a fishmonger, when not at school. One day on his rounds he saw a motorcycle in a field all in pieces, probably something like the photograph on the next page. He obtained this and with absolutely no experience whatsoever he put it together into a working machine. I don't know whether he got a road licence but it was possible at that time to get a licence aged 14. By the age of 17 he was a member of the Herne Bay Motorcycle Club.

Motorbike in parts (copyright Allan Ford)

Despite his lack of a good education, although he could read and write, my father was an unbelievably practical and capable man. During his life, right up until he was eighty, and without a single lesson or course in his life, he taught himself the mechanics of a motorbike, how to ride the Wall of Death, how to repair old vehicles (lorries and cars), how to build a caravan, how to restore and repair condemned *c.*1700 buildings, to build houses, to brick-lay (he taught me too). He could sail, ski, horse-ride and water-ski. He could repair any electrical faults, most gas and water faults, any motor car and motorbike. He could restore and make window frames, and restore chimneys, old flint work and brickwork, and build a garden swimming pool – long before they were commonplace.

He taught himself eventually to be a cabinet maker, to restore antique furniture and antique stone garden ornaments, to make glass chandeliers (he taught me too), to carve wood, to make furniture, and to make reproduction antique furniture. However, despite many trips to the Continent, he could not speak a word of German or French.

Unlike my mother, however, he did not keep press cuttings or photos of his career before he met my mother. In a BBC radio recording in the 1950s my father stated that he had started riding the Wall of Death in 1929, aged 19. I suspect he and his three brothers had seen the June 1929 Wall of Death at the Kursaal in Southend and realized they could become riders. It is also possible that my grandfather had some side stalls at the Kursaal. Also in 1924, aged 14, my father went on a school visit to the Wembley Exhibition in London, where he possibly saw the motorcyclists on The Death Ring.

By late 1929 my father was riding a wall, along with his older brother, Bob Todd, although the first newspaper report was in October 1930. I suspect he taught himself to ride the wall.

By 1932 at the age of 22 he was riding his Wall of Death in Ramsgate, Kent, at Merrie England amusement park along with his three brothers, Jack, Bob and Frank. The four brothers owned the wall between them and apparently it had been built by a Ramsgate boat-builder, although I have never been able to confirm that. The wall was called the 'Original Drome of Thrills'.

The Original Drome of Thrills, Ramsgate, 1932

The brothers had commercial postcards printed (shown on the next page), which they sold as souvenirs. The ones I have show Jack Todd, riding an Austin 7 tourer car, Jack and George racing each other, and my father towing Bob, who is on roller skates. This roller-skating act was already quite famous and although I think there was one other rider who did this stunt, it was quite rare. They spent the whole of the summer season of 1932 at Ramsgate.

Also with them at this stage was a Swiss lady rider, Gertrud Rodel, who later married Bob Todd, although I am not sure whether she was then riding the wall or they were teaching her. Also there was Miss Vivienne, a rider who later married Frank Todd.

Their barker on the bally was George Purser, a Ramsgate man, who was eventually a member of the Midland section of the Showmen's Guild. In 1999 his wife wrote to me to say how much her husband had enjoyed working for the Todd brothers and when he eventually retired he was a frequent visitor to my father, where they would, as she said, 'trip down memory lane'.[1]

The rest of my father's story is in separate chapters.

Frank Todd driving car, 1932

George Todd towing Bod Todd on skates, 1932

1. Letter from Lydia Purser to the author, 7 January 1999.

George Todd and Jack Todd racing, 1932

Chapter 12
Robert Todd, My Uncle, Known as Bob.

Born: 1901, Birmingham, UK. Married: Gertrud Rodel,
1936 in Blean, Kent.

Died: 1956, London. No children.

Rode the wall from 1929 until the Second World War. Was also on roller skates being towed behind his brothers' bikes.

Riding name: Initially Fearless Bob Todd, Fearless Death Rider, Dare-Devil Bob Todd then Bob Todd.

The oldest of the Todd brothers, Uncle Bob started riding the wall late in 1929, riding for Joe Silverstone. Silverstone, from South Africa, worked for Silodrome Pty Ltd. and it was that company who was responsible for the 1929 first appearances at Manchester and at the Kursaal, Southend. This would seem to support my theory that all four Todd brothers visited the wall at the Kursaal to see what all the fuss was about! Whilst riding for Silverstone Bob came up with the idea of using roller skates and being towed behind Joe's bike. After several attempts leading to crashes he replaced the roller skate steel wheels with rubber ones, no longer crashed, and perfected his act. As a teenager he had been a member of the Folkestone Roller Skating Hockey Club, so was already a roller skater. His roller-skating act became quite famous and he was the first to perform the act.

By 1930 Bob Todd, calling himself the Fearless Death Rider, was leader of a team on one of Pat Collins' Death Rider teams. My father, George Todd, was probably also a member. In October they performed at Fazeley Statute Fair in Tamworth and it was reported: 'Bob Todd the Fearless

Death Rider is leader of the team and the sensation of the fair and the district in general. Bob Todd was the admiration of all who saw him.'[1]

Bob in Folkestone roller-skating team

At the same time, when not riding, Bob was running an antique shop in Whitstable, Kent, probably in partnership with my grandparents.

Uncle Bob and my father continued to tour the UK in 1931 but in 1932 all four of the brothers appeared at Merrie England in Ramsgate, covered in Chapter 11. By then Bob was thirty-one. Once the season finished he formed a duo with my father in 1933, covered in Chapter 15. By 1934 he owned a wall which he then took to Italy, where Frank, his brother, had already been since late 1929.

In April 1934 in Turin Bob and his brother Frank rode together and Bob performed his roller-skating act and the two of them also wore crash helmets. By this time Bob had replaced the rope he used in the roller-skating act in Ramsgate in 1932 with a steel handle attached to his brother's motorbike. That was fortunate for although they both crashed and were taken to hospital, they were not seriously hurt. The episode was reported in the *Kokomo Tribune* in America.[2]

Bob's wall in Italy, 1930s

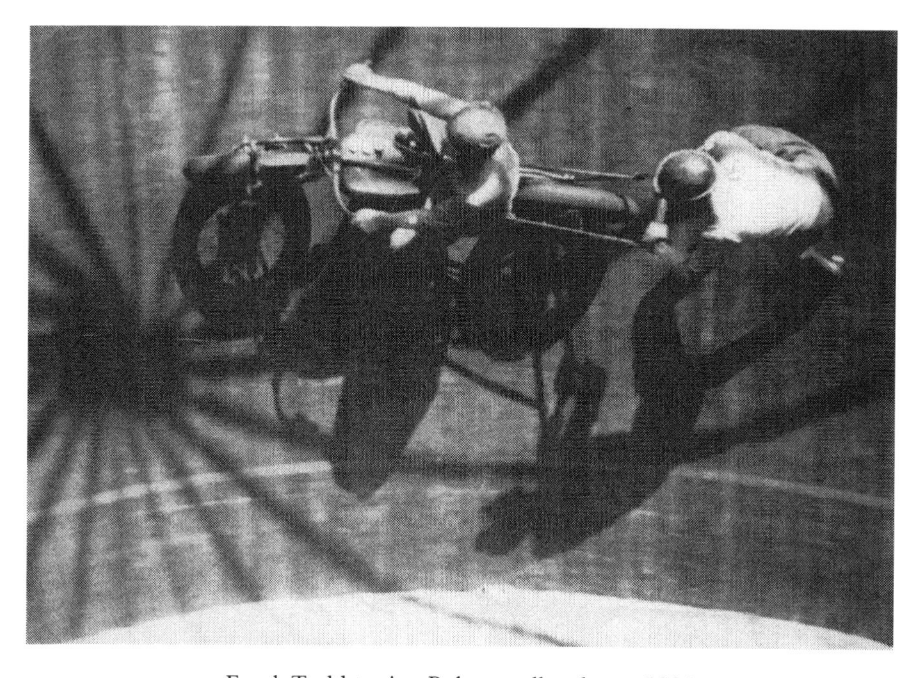

Frank Todd towing Bob on roller skates, 1934

Later in 1934 Bob returned to the UK with Trude Rodel and they started riding with his brother Jack. Jack placed an advert in the paper announcing: 'The Original Drome of Thrills is open to proposition – 100 per cent act consists of car, roller skater and super motorcycle act'. The photo shows the wall frontage with Jack, Bob and Trude Rodel.[3]

Jack and Bod Todd with Trude

In 1936 Bob married Gertrud Rodel (Trude), a Swiss lady, who by then was a Wall of Death rider, and whom he had known since the early thirties. He put his profession down on the marriage certificate as antique dealer and not Wall of Death rider. In fact none of the wedding certificates of the Todd brothers lists their profession or their wives' as Wall of Death rider. Maybe there was a list of professions one could choose from and a Wall of Death rider was not one of them!

Early in 1939 Bob and Trude and my mother and father bought a Wall of Death, called the Hell Drivers, covered in Chapter 17.

---

1. *The World's Fair,* 11 October 1930.
2. *The Kokomo Tribune,* 30 April 1934.
3. *The World's Fair,* 14 April 1934.

Chapter 13

Frank Todd, My Uncle

Born: 1906, Birmingham, UK. Married: Ethel Boustead, (known as Miss Vivienne), 1950. Died: 1981, London.
Son: Franco Todd, born Genoa, Italy, 1932.
Rider Name: Only ever rode as Frank Todd. Rode from 1929 until 1953.

Frank left school in Folkestone, Kent, and went into his father's antique business to learn the trade. His first foray into show business was when he built a sideshow called Australian Fruit Game (Cop-a-Lot) which he ran in London.

Having seen the 1929 Wall of Death at the Kursaal he built his own wall in Hounslow in partnership with Mark Lloyd and Count de Brassy, Frank teaching himself to ride. He left his partners and went to France where he rode the wall of Brown and Provatio for six months. The wall then went to the Lido, Milan. This was an Australian wall and Frank rode before the Italian Royal Family there. It moved to Naples where he rode before Italy's famous flyer, General Balbo.

Australian Wall in Turin, 1930

Whilst in Italy Frank met Alec Hurley, who was touring but not riding a Silodrome. The two became partners and built a wall and Frank taught Alec to ride. The wall was called *Muro Della Morte.* Hurley was never too keen on riding and eventually sold his share to Frank, who was still driving his adapted Austin 7 tourer car. He also had a lion on the wall, although I have no photos of that – it did escape once into a milk bar.

Muro Della Morte wall bally with Frank and car, Alec Hurley and Miss Vivienne

Alec Hurley, Frank Todd in car, Miss Vivienne

Frank Todd's wall, *Muro Della Morte*

Apart from driving a car Frank was also a skilled trick rider and I have several photos of him doing tricks, the best of which has one leg in the air. The car photo is also the one printed in *The World's Fair* 1953 article.

Frank Todd trick riding

Frank Todd in car, Italy

In 1932 Frank returned to England to ride with his three brothers in Ramsgate, Kent, covered in Chapter 11. In November he sent a photo of his Italian wall to *The World's Fair* and it was printed, with the caption:

> Frank Todd's Wall of Death has been touring Italy for the last three years and is still doing good business. Our picture shows from left to right A. Hurley, Italian spieler, Vivienne Johnson (in car) and Frank Todd.[1]

On returning to Italy with Miss Vivienne in 1932 their son Franco was born.

> All sorts of things happened thereafter in a land changing its way of life to suit the whims of a dictator and Fascism. A performance was given to that leader of the Blackshirts, Mussolini. At another time the Fascists closed the show down as not being good for the Italian public. Frank was chased by Benito's disciples and had to hide for three or four days to escape castor oil 'treatment' and attentions of the lictor.[2]

Before returning to England again in 1936, in that year he took his wall to Abyssinia, which was then occupied by the Italians.

'When in Abyssinia he found that the locals prayed for him as he took the lions round on the wall'.[3]

On returning to England he opened a performing monkey circus and toured the Midlands. He then took his wall to Egypt.

Frank Todd and his monkey circus

On returning to Italy again: 'This time he was more fortunate and the Italian "Showmen's Guild" made him an honorary member with a permit to go where he liked without reporting to the authorities.'[4]

On 9 May 1939 Frank, Vivienne and their son were still in Italy. However, things became very difficult because of the approaching war – Frank eventually fled Italy, leaving behind his wall, his car, motorbikes and lorries. He may have lost everything.

By December 1939 he was back in the UK where he attended the wedding of one of his sisters, together with Vivienne and their son. He also built another wall in the UK.

He certainly seems to have had an unusual time in his ten years in Italy, building yet another wall, riding before famous people, being hounded by the Fascists, learning Italian and finally being made an honorary member of the Italian Showmen's Guild. It is also clear from his photo album that he appeared in many Italian cities – unfortunately they are not all named and there are no dates.

What Frank did during the war is in Chapter 18 and after the war in Chapter 22.

---

1. *The World's Fair,* 12 November 1932.
2. Ibid., 25 July 1953.
3. Ibid.
4. Ibid.

Chapter 14
Gertrud Rodel and Ethel Boustead, My Aunts by Marriage

Born: Gertrud Rodel, 1916, St. Galen, Switzerland.
Married: Robert Todd in 1936. Died: unknown.
No children.
Riding name: Trude Rodel, Senorita Trude.
Rode in the UK from 1932 till 1939.

Trude first appeared in 1932 in Merrie England, Ramsgate, where the four Todd brothers were riding the wall. Bob of course was doing his roller-skating act. There are no 1932 photos of Trude riding the wall but one person from Ramsgate,[1] who saw their show, told me that there was also a learner lady roller skater and I presume it was Trude – but there are no reports of her skating on a wall.

When my father and Bob rode together round Britain between 1930 and 1933, Trude does not appear to have been in their show. However, she was clearly around because in 1936 she married Bob in Kent, giving her address as my Todd family home in Whitstable.

In late 1938 or early 1939 she and Bob and my mother and father had a wall built (Chapter 17). When my mother and father bought them out Trude and Bob appeared together at Barnstaple Fair in late 1939 on Grant's wall.

Bob Todd and Trude on rollers, 1930

* * *

Born: Ethel Bousted, always known as Miss Vivienne, 1907.
Married: Frank Todd Senior, 1950. Later divorced.
Died: Jersey, unknown date. Son: Franco Todd, born 1932 in Genoa.
Riding name: Miss Vivienne. Rode in UK and Italy – 1930–1939.

Before meeting Uncle Frank, Vivienne had ridden with Al Johnson, whom she married but later left and then divorced.

In May 1930 she was photographed with Al Johnson on the front of the Anderton and Rowlands Death Ride in Plymouth and the photo appeared in *The World's Fair.* My own photograph shows her and other riders sitting on the front of Anderton and Rowland's wall.[2]

Anderton and Rowland's Big Show – Miss Vivienne in fur collar

In September 1930 she and Al appeared at Barnstaple Fair where she was advertised as Miss Vivienne, the third rider being Cyclone Campbell.

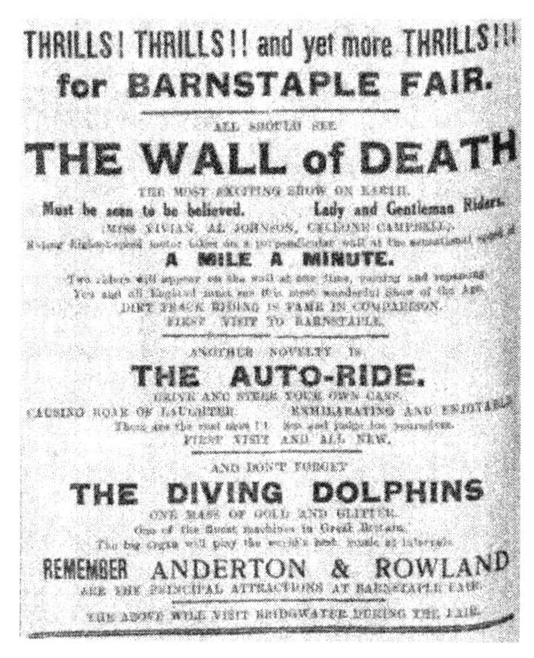

Advert Barnstaple –
The Wall of Death

In 1931 they appeared at Canterbury Carnival Week on the Drome of Death.

Drome of Death, Miss Vivienne on wall

Thereafter she left Al Johnson and rode with Frank Todd Senior, eventually marrying him. I have dozens of photographs of her riding with Frank in Italy.

---

1. Letter from B. Wallis in Margate to author.
2. *The World's Fair*, 10 May 1930.

Chapter 15

George and Bob Todd, Fearless Egbert and the Lions, 1933

Early in 1933, after leaving Merrie England in Ramsgate, my father and Uncle Bob starting riding for the showman Jack Barry on his wall, which he called Barry's Sensational Wall of Death Show. Jack Barry had been a wall rider previously but did not ride on his own wall. My father and Uncle Bob rode together for the whole of 1933.

Appearing with them was Ferald Eugene Egbert (Fearless Egbert). Egbert was an American born in 1897, so he was already thirty-six when he appeared with my father and uncle. He had already toured the Continent with his act by 1927, when he returned to America from France. He then arrived in the UK in December 1930 and toured his act throughout Britain on one of the walls owned by the showman Collins. He was very famous, for he rode a car which he had built himself, which had an Indian twin-cylinder engine. At the side of the car was a platform and Egbert travelled with one of two lions, called Monarch and Briton. Egbert allowed one lion to jump onto the platform and then drove the car round the Wall of Death. The lion was not strapped on at all.

Fearless Egbert in car with lion

The lions took it in turns to be the 'passenger'. The first time the lion ever went on the wall he enjoyed it so much he refused to get off. When Egbert appeared at Hull in 1931 it was reported that 35,000 people had seen the show.

In 1931 a long article appeared entitled 'Egbert and Monarch the Lion's special relationship':

> It is remarkable how even lions can become civilized. Three years ago, Monarch the lion, that will ride on a baby car around a wall at Woodhouse Feast, had never seen a motor car. … [In America] on seeing a baby car which is driven by Fearless Egbert he clambered into it. When he was given a ride he enjoyed it so much he refused to get out. … Monarch was gradually introduced to the thrills in a car around a vertical wall. … If Egbert stops the car too soon, the young lion remains on the car. … when he gets a little bored, and the driver knows it is time to stop when he realizes that Monarch's head is very close to his face.[1]

At the Preston Whit Fair in June 1933, on for four days, my father and Uncle Bob and Egbert were advertised as:

> First Visit to Preston of Barry's Sensational Wall of Death Show. The Greatest Show Ever Seen in Great Britain featuring motor-racing lions and motor-car stunting, Dare-Devil Bob Todd roller skating 20 foot in the air and George Todd and his hair-raising stunts on a motorcycle.[2]

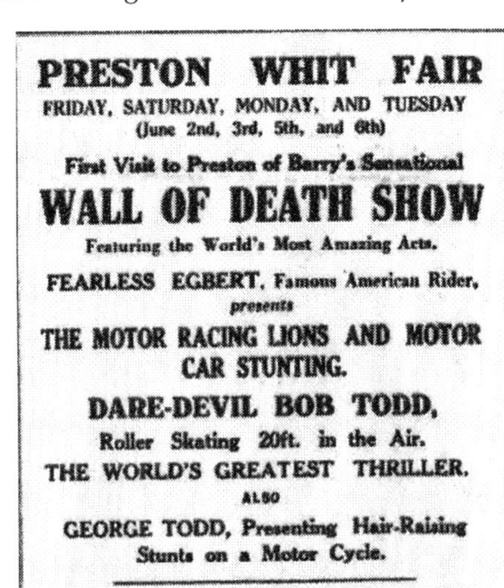

Preston Whit Fair, 1933

However, my father had an accident at this fair, skidding on the bike and falling from it, although he was not badly hurt. It was reported in several newspapers.

By July the act appeared for the first time ever in Scotland, at Gussie Park in Dundee, where my uncle's roller-skating act was a great attraction. A newspaper noted:

> Notable among the many hair-raising stunts which will be performed by a crack team of trick riders is Dare Devil Bob Todd's roller-skating act 20 feet in the air. Motor car stunts are included in the repertoire, and Fearless Egbert and his motor-racing lions, while additional cycle thrills will be supplied by George Todd.[3]

Gussie Park, 1933

By September 1933 Egbert seems to have temporally left the act, probably to visit his American family. My father and uncle appeared in Lincoln in September for five days and were advertised as 'The Original Wall of Death'.[4]

In October they were in Hull, where my father was described as:

> … a famous London dirt-track rider, who will be making his first appearance at the fair, presenting amazing stunts of high speed motor cycling round the perpendicular walls. His stunts are sufficient to appease the thirst of thrill seekers.[5]

Also, his car caught fire in the street in Hull. The car was being driven by Jake Messham, whom my father was probably training. The Messhams went on to become a family dynasty of wall riders and owners, and their descendants still run two walls and a globe today, and, incidentally, live only ten minutes away from me.

Whilst there are few newspaper reports my father and Uncle Bob toured the whole of England and Scotland in 1933.

---

1. *Yorkshire Evening Post*, 24 September 1931 (reproduced with kind permission of the British Newspaper Archive, www.britishnewspaperarchive.co.uk).
2. *Lancashire Evening Post*, 1 June 1933 (reproduced with kind permission of the British Newspaper Archive, www.britishnewspaperarchive.co.uk).
3. *Evening Telegraph*, 28 July 1933 (reproduced with kind permission of the British Newspaper Archive, www.britishnewspaperarchive.co.uk).
4. *Lincolnshire Echo*, 25 September 1933 (reproduced with kind permission of the British Newspaper Archive, www.britishnewspaperarchive.co.uk).
5. *Hull Daily Mail*, 11 October 1933 (reproduced with kind permission of the British Newspaper Archive, www.britishnewspaperarchive.co.uk).

Chapter 16

Wyn and George Todd, Fearless Egbert, the Lions and a Monkey, 1934–1938

After he rode for Jack Barry in 1933, Barry employed my father again at the beginning of 1934 and in March advertised in *The World's Fair* for a lady rider.[1]

My mother answered this advert and she too was employed by Barry, along with my father, Fearless Egbert and his lions. During the year Harry Greenslade and Jack O'Malley rode for him and in 1935 Speedy Brum (Francis C. Birmingham) joined the team permanently.

At this time my mother changed her riding name from Fearless Winnie to Miss Winifred Soutter and was sometimes advertised as 'England's Champion Lady Rider'.

Barry's Super Wall of Death Show

Barry's wall was either called 'Barry's Sensational Lion Motordrome', 'Barry's Super Wall of Death Show presenting Motor Racing Lions', 'Barry's Hell Drivers' or 'The World's Greatest Wall of Death'. The paintings on the outside of the wall, the name of the wall and the notices on the bally were frequently changed over the years.

Fearless Egbert and his racing lions were already famous and the photo of Barry's Super Wall of Death Show, in Manchester, features Fearless Egbert, Jack O'Malley, Winifred Soutter and George Todd and the lions' cage on the bally.

For the next five years my mother and father stayed with Barry's wall, together with Egbert and his lions and Speedy Brum. Barry's wall appeared all over the country from 1934 to 1938 – from Scotland to Kent, the North of England to the West Country. Barry was a member of the Showmen's Guild and therefore had access to all fairs, most importantly the great traditional fairs of Britain, which were given charters in the Medieval period. These included Barnstaple, Cambridge Mid-Summer, Hull Annual, King's Lynn, Newcastle Town Moor, Oxford St Giles, Stratford on Avon Mop, Warwick Mop, Nottingham Goose Fair, Knutsford May, Kirkcaldy Links Market, Newcastle Town Moor and Loughborough. It was at Loughborough, Dudley Carnival, Nottingham Goose Fair and Hull that Uncle Jack Todd first rode in 1929. From there on, there was a wall at all of these fairs. Many old photographs of fairs show hundreds if not thousands of people milling around the fairgrounds.

Harry Allen painting, 1934
(copyright Geraldine Latley)

Early in 1934 the Yorkshire artist Harry E. Allen painted a picture of a Wall of Death. Allen's office was opposite the Sheffield fairground, which he would have been able to see from his windows. The painting was then exhibited at the Royal Society of British Artists in London in April 1934. It now hangs in the Laing Gallery, Newcastle. Apparently he left no records of whose wall this was.

In June of that year after a wall appeared at Nottingham, local lads used a dried-up pond, fifty yards in circumference, as a makeshift Wall of Death.[2]

Egbert's two lions were called Jimmy and Rex and I believe my father occasionally took the lion up for a public show, and my parents also did so privately, without an audience. My father, however, was the man who usually led the lions into the wall.

In May they appeared at Preston Whit Fair, and were called 'Barry's Sensational Wall of Death Show'. In June they appeared again at Preston, in July at Doncaster and in August at Himslet. These were the only appearances reported in the newspapers. They actually worked every week, travelling from fair to fair.

In September 1934 at Armley Feast Fair two episodes took place involving my father and the other riders, which reached all the local newspapers. On Saturday 1 September, as usual my father opened the door for the two lions to come into the wall, armed with a chair, an iron long fork and a stick for protection. What then happened was that one lion returned through a tunnel to its cage, whilst the other lion went on the wall, but on this occasion the second lion returned into the wall from its cage. The two lions got stroppy – Rex refused to return to his cage and started stalking Egbert along with Jimmy and both became aggressive. My father and Harry Greenslade tried to keep the lions away from Egbert and get them to return to their cage. The lions became very aggressive for fifteen minutes, roaring and snarling and swiping the chairs the men held for protection. Eventually the three exhausted and frightened men called for three ladders to be let down into the wall so they could get out. When the first ladder was dropped into the wall it frightened the lions, who then returned to their cage.[3]

It happened again on Monday 3 September. Rex got onto the side platform of the car and Jimmy returned to his cage. Egbert then went into the cage to bring Jimmy out but got followed by Rex into the cage. Harry Greenslade then entered the cage but the lions swung at them with their claws and Greenslade was trapped in the corner. O'Malley pushed a wooden guard between Greenslade and the lions. The lions returned to the inside of the wall but again became aggressive and when ladders were dropped they took no notice of them but eventually returned to their cage. Some time during these two events Rex did try to bite Egbert, for the first time ever. Also one of the lions destroyed one of the chairs the riders were using for protection. Eventually both lions were in their cage again. The show carried on afterwards as normal. The audience probably thought it was all part of the act. I am, however, very surprised that my mother did not insist that they no longer rode on that wall with the lions.[4]

There were complaints to the newspapers about cruelty to lions and Egbert replied and put forward his case saying the problem was that one of the lions liked riding the wall so much it always wanted to go up.

There was an added problem in that their cage faced a scary sideshow opposite, with a big model of a 10-foot-long bright red dragon which revolved, at the same time emitting weird screeching sounds. Egbert came to the conclusion that this had upset the lions, since in his four years of working with them they had never behaved in such an aggressive manner. He did decide, however, not to have the lions together inside the wall again and to buy a gun. It appears that this alarming behaviour never happened again once they left that fairground.[5]

Egbert once stated that the lions had no teeth and before a ride he fed them on Hovis bread soaked in Guinness. The heavy brown bread and the Guinness made the lion very sleepy. Egbert also stated that the worst thing was when a lion farted – the audience did not like the bad smell!

At some stage during this period Barry also had a monkey in the act, which drove a very small car round the wall. The monkey belonged to Alfred John North, himself a rider. It was called Jacko and occasionally escaped and on one occasion had to be rescued by the fire brigade because it got stuck up a tree. Personally I thought monkeys lived in trees! I have a photograph of my parents on the front of the wall, together with the monkey in his little car, Egbert and the lions' cage, and the other rider. That show including lions, a monkey and the riders must have been quite a sensation. Allan Ford maintains that by the mid-1930s there were about fifty walls operating in Britain, so to include something special was an added attraction both for the audience and for the showmen who controlled the fairs.

A Mr Geoffrey Wood once reported that late in 1929 he and his father Tim Wood went to see a Wall of Death at Olympia in Bradford. His father was talked into having a go on the wall (he had won the TT in 1913 riding an Indian Scout). He had no difficulty in doing a straight ride on the wall. So the owners then produced a motorbike with an open side car for him to ride – they also produced a real live full-grown Bengal tiger. Tim managed to drive the car and the tiger – his wife, however, was not impressed and it appears that Tim and she separated and his son never saw his father again.[6] Early in the 1930s one couple of riders also took a brown bear on the wall and another trained a dog.

America's Sensational Act, lion cage, Egbert, Winifred Soutter,
George Todd and monkey in car

Some time in 1934 Pathé News filmed Barry's wall and Egbert and the lions, which was, presumably, shown on the news in cinemas. My father is the man holding the door open for the lions to enter. The film then shows Egbert taking the lion on the wall. My father can also be seen looking down into the wall from the walkround once he had closed the lions' entry door and the performance started. This must have been quite a publicity coup for the show.[7]

George Todd leading Jimmy and Rex into the wall
(British Pathé, http://www.britishpathé.com)

In September thousands saw their act in Hastings.[8] In October 1934 they appeared first in Houghton and then at Hull Annual Fair when Barry called the show 'The World's Greatest Wall of Death'. In December they were at Selby and Wombwell. At this stage my mother was being advertised as 'Miss Winifred Soutter, England's Champion Lady Rider' on The World's Greatest Wall of Death.[9]

In late December and early January 1935 they appeared at the Agricultural Halls in London, where my father had an accident and broke his arm. Fearless Egbert helped prevent a worse accident as he pulled my father out of the way of the falling motorbike. It was also reported that one of my father's tricks was to ride round with the lion in the sidecar.[10]

In May 1935, my parents got married in Bromley, Kent, where my mother's parents lived. My mother was only twenty and my father twenty-six. Each gave their address as their parents' homes. My father put his profession down as a motor mechanic and my mother left the space blank. Fearless Egbert was a wedding guest. My mother still used her riding name, Miss Winifred Soutter. After their marriage they acquired a caravan, either bought or perhaps built by my father.

Wedding of Wyn Soutter and George Todd, 1935

Wall riders did not take holidays at Christmas, New Year and Easter or between spring and late summer – they were always working. So my parents, who were of course extremely fit and healthy, looked for an unusual late-winter holiday and spent their honeymoon in Grindelwald,

Switzerland, learning to ski. It was one of the very first package ski tours. They clearly enjoyed skiing for, apart from the war years, they skied for the rest of the lives until their deaths aged 73 and 80.

Wyn Todd outside of caravan, 1930s

In June 1935 they appeared at Preston Whit Fair again where my mother was billed as:

> The World's Greatest Lady Trick Motorcyclist in Sensational Acts, George Todd and Speedy Brum presenting Hair-Raising Stunts on a Motorcycle and The Amazing 'Race Of Death', The Greatest Show Ever Seen in Great Britain.[11]

The paper later reported:

> The Wall of Death never seems to lose its thrill in drawing large crowds. The two motor-racing lions show their skill in riding a small racing car and Fearless Egbert, the American rider, is hero once more. Miss Winnie Soutter performs some sensational tricks and George Todd and Speedy Brum take part in hair-raising tricks.[12]

Amongst other places they appeared at Stamford Mid-Lent and Stevenage fairs, Newcastle, Wakefield, Durham Miners Gala, Driffield, Peterborough and Birmingham.

In July they were widely advertised as 'the first visit of Barry's Sensational Lion Motordrome to Newcastle, with Fearless Egbert and the world-famous wall riders Miss Winifred Soutter, George Todd and Speedy Birmingham'. It was advertised in many parts of the district.[13]

In October they were in Peterborough and The Hull Annual Fair.

> Fearless Egbert, the famous American dare devil, takes a full grown lion for a ride in a motor car at Barry's Lion Motordrome, but this is one of many acts. A team of riders race on the Wall of Death with motor cars and motorcycles, among the artistes being Miss Winifred Soutter, Great Britain's Champion lady motorcyclist, George Todd and Speedy Brum. Todd and Brum are trick acrobatic cyclists, whose high speed feats are simply amazing. Anyone in search of a thrill will find it here, for three motorcyclists dash round the wall at the same time in a sensational race of death.[14]

During 1936 they still appeared all over the country, including Bury Fair, Huddersfield (where they were very well advertised locally), Newark, Newcastle, Nelson, Hull, Huddersfield, Bradford, Ilkley, Tonbridge, Leeds and York.

At Halifax Spring Fair It was reported that:

> Barry's Wall of Death has long been recognized as one of the finest exhibitions of its kind. The programme is given in a well-lit wall and opens with the renowned Egbert riding round in a 4-wheel car with a full grown lion and Miss Soutter provides a good turn with her clever trick riding – one spin being within an inch or two of the safety mark at the top of the wall and the next one being at the bottom.
>
> The climax is when three riders are racing round at once – they zigzag in all directions and provide thrills, which the audience appear to appreciate.[15]

By September in Tonbridge Barry called the team 'Barry's Famous Hell Drivers and Racing Lions, Miss Winifred Soutter, Great Britain's Champion Lady Motorcyclist, with George Todd and Speedy Brum, Trick and Acrobatic Motorcyclists and Featuring Fearless Egbert and his lion'.[16]

The October Hull Annual Fair, where they appeared, was one of the biggest in Europe with 200 living wagons, 160 lorries and 186 shows on 13 acres of land. So there was plenty of competition.

There is no doubt that the Wall of Death was becoming extremely popular with the public. In 1936 the town council of Wisbech discussed whether to ban walls from their fairground. There was some discussion about whether it was dangerous – it was decided it was not. However,

George and Wynn Todd, Speedy Brum in car, Egbert

much more significant is that there was great discussion about the fact that the wall was so popular that the crowds were going into the wall rather than spending money on other fairground shows. It was decided by the council that it was, in fact, a good thing to have such a popular show at the fair because it drew in more of the public, and after a discussion as to whether the council should charge a higher rent to Wall of Death owners, because they took more money, it was decided not to do so. They also decided that walls could be present on their fairground.[17]

During 1936 there were eleven walls touring, including Jack Barry with my parents and Jack and Bob Todd's wall. For four weeks over Christmas 1936 and New Year the 'Hell Drivers' appeared at the Agricultural Halls in London. They also were there over the Christmas/New Year period in 1937 and 1938. Their wall continued to appear all over Britain and was widely advertised.

In July at Buxton they were 'the talk of the town and they should be congratulated on such a fine exhibit which includes lions, Miss Winifred Soutter, Speedy Brum and George Todd'.[18]

At Barnstaple Fair a member of the public wrote in complaining about lions on the wall. At Hull in October the King and Queen apparently saw the show. At Grantham Mid-Lent Fair Barry's Wall of Death was, apparently, the most important show.

PUBLIC NOTICES

BARRY'S

HELL DRIVERS AND RACING LIONS

FEATURING

FEARLESS EGBERT

THE FAMOUS AMERICAN RIDER, WHO TAKES A LION FOR A RIDE ON A MOTOR CAR, AROUND THE WALL OF DEATH

AND

THE WORLD'S GREATEST WALL OF DEATH RIDERS

MISS WINIFRED SOUTTER,

GEORGE TODD, SPEEDY BRUM.

SEE THE SENSATIONAL RACE OF DEATH

THREE RIDERS ON THE WALL AT ONE TIME.

DIRT TRACK MIDGET CAR RACING ON THE STRAIGHT WALL.

THE MOST SENSATIONAL PERFORMANCE EVER PRESENTED IN GREAT BRITAIN.

DON'T FAIL TO VISIT THE SHOW WHICH IS THE TALK OF THE COUNTRY.

Barry's Hell Drivers and Racing Lions, press cutting, 1937

Speedy Brum was still part of the team after five years. Towards the end of 1938 Egbert left the show for good to perform once again in America, probably fearing the onset of war in Europe. He returned in 1939 to work for John Collins but left at the end of the year for America.

During the 1930s riders often changed riding partners and they often rode for different Wall of Death owners. Owners sometimes sold their walls, sometimes advertised to buy one, and frequently advertised for wall riders. Not all riders were good ones. Several only rode for very short periods; several had bad accidents and had to stop.

The fact that my parents rode for Jack Barry for six years, and with the same team, indicates that this team worked very well together and all got on extremely well. They trusted each other as riders – something which was extremely important on a wall, where the slightest mistake could mean an accident or, even worse, death. They were also clearly reliable and, according to numerous newspaper reports, highly skilled and presented an outstanding show. They also obviously maintained their machines properly (also extremely important). There was no other report of a team staying together for so many years.

As for cruelty to animals – in 1938 the RSPCA prosecuted Alfred North for cruelty for taking a monkey on the wall and he was fined.

Also in 1938, at the AGM of the RSPCA the matter of cruelty to lions on the wall was discussed. Sir Robert Gower MP, presiding, replied, 'it would be useless to bring a case to the courts as it was impossible to prove cruelty. A veterinary surgeon of the society had examined the animal in question and found it in splendid condition and with no possible evidence of any cruelty'. The same vet actually went on the wall, in place of the lion, and reported back to the RSPCA:

> I took the place of the lion, and I may say that I did so with some trepidation. I had a handkerchief in my hand so that if I felt at all peculiar I could drop it. After I had gone round once, however, I felt quite confident, and I put the handkerchief away. I did not have the slightest sensation of falling off or as if I was going to fall off. When I had finished I walked straight off and was able to keep a straight line.

He reported back that riding the Wall of Death was quite pleasant and in no way could it be construed a cruelty to the lions. Egbert, therefore, was neither fined nor prosecuted.[19]

During 1938 a female member of the audience fell on the walkround on John Collins wall and sued John Collins for damages but she lost. At the court hearing Collins stated that since the accident 93,000 people had seen his wall and there had not been one accident. This is another example of the numbers of people flocking to see the sensational shows.[20]

By this time the Wall of Death was suitable material for children to read about. A strip cartoon called 'About a Wall of Death' appeared in a local paper.[21]

---

1. *The World's Fair,* 10 March 1934.
2. *Nottingham Evening Post,* 18 June 1934 (reproduced with kind permission of the British Newspaper Archive, www.britishnewspaperarchive.co.uk).
3. *Sunderland Daily Echo,* 3 September 1934 (reproduced with kind permission of the British Newspaper Archive, www.britishnewspaperarchive.co.uk).
4. *Yorkshire Evening Post,* 3 September 1934 (reproduced with kind permission of the British Newspaper Archive, www.britishnewspaperarchive.co.uk).
5. Ibid., 7 September 1934.
6. *Vintage Sports Car Club,* undated but after 1993.
7. See Britishpathe.com/video/taking a lion for a ride.
8. *Hastings & St Leonards Observer,* 8 September 1934.

9. Advertisement, *Hull Daily Mail*, 12 October 1934 (reproduced with kind permission of the British Newspaper Archive, www.britishnewspaperarchive.co.uk).
10. *The World's Fair*, 19 January 1935, front page.
11. Advertisement, *Lancashire Evening Post*, 7 June 1935 (reproduced with kind permission of the British Newspaper Archive, www.britishnewspaperarchive.co.uk).
12. Ibid., 8 June 1935.
13. *The World's Fair*, 20 July 1935.
14. *Hull Daily Mail*, 10 October 1935 (reproduced with kind permission of the British Newspaper Archive, www.britishnewspaperarchive.co.uk).
15. *The World's Fair*, 4 April 1936.
16. Advertisement, *Kent & Sussex Courier*, 18 September 1936 (reproduced with kind permission of the British Newspaper Archive, www.britishnewspaperarchive.co.uk).
17. *The World's Fair*, 1 February 1936.
18. Ibid., 3 July 1937.
19. *Kent & Sussex Courier*, 27 May 1938 (reproduced with kind permission of the British Newspaper Archive, www.britishnewspaperarchive.co.uk).
20. *Dundee Evening Telegraph*, 25 October 1938 (reproduced with kind permission of the British Newspaper Archive, www.britishnewspaperarchive.co.uk).
21. *Gloucester Journal*, 31 December 1938 (reproduced with kind permission of the British Newspaper Archive, www.britishnewspaperarchive.co.uk).

Chapter 17

The Hell Drivers, Wyn and George Todd and Bob and Trude Todd, 1939

Early in 1939 my parents decided to buy their own Wall of Death together with my uncle and aunt, Bob and Trude Todd. Bob and Trude had obviously come back from Italy. They had a wall built by a boat-builder in Ramsgate, Kent, probably the same man who built the 1932 one for the four Todd brothers. At that time a wall made of eighteen wooden sections cost about £750. They would also, of course, have had to buy the lorries for transporting the wall, so it was quite a financial commitment. My parents certainly did not borrow money to acquire their wall, for my father never bought anything at all on credit all his life, so between the four of them they must have saved up the money. This was quite a risky decision at that particular time – it was becoming increasingly possible that war would break out, which would, no doubt, have quite a negative impact on fairs and fairgrounds. There was also the added problem that none of them were members of the Showmen's' Guild.

The new wall was up and running by February at Oswestry, where George and Bob Todd were the star performers and the spieler was Jack Lancaster, who was probably living with my aunt, Gladys Restall.[1]

At Shrewsbury a week later Bob gave an interview explaining how he started the roller-skating act (see Chapter 12).

The guild, started in 1889, had fairly strict codes of operation and held a very important controlling position regarding who could appear at fairs. My father had tried to join the guild but its rules meant that he was not qualified, for the guild was only open to members whose families were showmen. My mother's family were not showmen and although my grandfather had a few side stalls on fairs, he was not considered to be a showman. So anyone who was not a member could only present a show with the permission of a Riding Master in charge of a particular fair, and this meant the vast majority of the fairs, and certainly included the numerous really famous annual ones like Nottingham Goose Fair.

However, my parents had been riding the wall for a decade by then and had made friends amongst the showmen and these included some famous ones like Pat Collins, Jack Barry, Billy Manning, Billy Smart, Bertram Mills and Billy Butlin. My uncle Jack Soutter pointed out that:

> They had a first-class show with a good reputation. By knowing the right people, with a lot of help from my sister's personality and her friendliness with the women folk of the top Riding Masters (Showmen), such as Billy Manning, the Codonas and Billy Smart and by approaching councils directly. They also talked to the smaller showmen in the right way, telling them how they would increase their own takings with the extra people the Wall of Death would bring to the fair.[2]

It would also seem that perhaps the guild were relaxing their rules somewhat for the wall which my parents and uncle and aunt owned did not always have a name on it associated with one of the guild showmen, as had previously been done.

The team of four called themselves the 'Hell Drivers 1939'. For the whole of 1939 it toured Britain. The wall itself was quite impressive. The bally was on top of the front; all four of the riders rode on the bally from time to time. The backdrop to the top bally was painted with a lady and a man rider on bikes. The name, Hell Drivers 1939, was made of light bulbs, which flashed on and off, and made the wall really stand out in the evening darkness. Below the name was sometimes a notice saying 'see the Human Fly skating 20 feet high'. The lower bally at the front stage was floodlit.

The Hell Drivers Team, as painted on the lower bally front, was Winifred Soutter, Trude Rodel and George and Bob Todd. The other painted notice stated it was the 'only wall of its kind with Roller Skating 20 foot high'. Along the bottom of the frontage was painted the word 'Sensational'.

Uncle Bob also had his car which he drove round the wall – I don't think he rode a bike on this wall – his act was the car and the roller skating. Their uniforms were white all-in-one overalls, together with calf-high leather boots. They rode Indian Scout motorbikes. They did not, however, have a lion or a monkey act.

Bob and Trude Todd, George and Wyn Todd

In April in Wrexham G.A. Robert reported:

> I was startled by a shattering roar of which I fondly imagined to be a ten ton tractor ... I found George Todd tuning up a midget car he is to take on the wall. It is named Billy Murden and number 113, painted a red with low slung bonnet ... the Todds go to Hampton Court next.[3]

However, I believe this was actually one of Billy Murden's cars, which my father bought. Murden was quite a well-known midget-car racer.

At Darleston in April it was reported:

> Hell Drivers are present and I was impressed by the smartness and efficiency of the riders. Bob's skating act is well put over and his brother George is riding better than ever.[4]

My father sent a copy of a photo to *The World's Fair,* which was printed on the front page with the caption:

> Hell Drivers of 1939. J. J. Collins show at Chester Race Fair, which was one of the biggest attractions. George and Bob Todd with their wives are seen in this sensational show.

Because the bally is 12' above the original stage riders can be seen from all parts of the ground.[5]

48 PAGES

THE WORLD'S FAIR

48 PAGES

"HELL DRIVERS OF 1939"

J. J. COLLINS'S SHOW AT CHESTER RACE FAIR

The World's Fair, May 1939
(copyright *The World's Fair*)

The Hell Drivers, George Todd on rollers

The Hell Drivers, Trude Todd on rollers

In May they appeared at Preston Whitsun Fair, and in September at Doncaster Fair my father was spieling, Trude was on the rollers and behind Uncle Bob you can just see the car.

They toured all through England all of that year, and would have been somewhere different every week and, in some cases, two different towns in one week. However, my mother had now been riding for nine years and I think she had stopped collecting press cuttings by this time, because there were very, very few in her papers, with the exception of this report of an interview with my mother:

> '... We've always been motorcycle conscious in my family,' explained Winifred, 'ten of them are now travelling all over the country or abroad in Wall of Death Acts.'
>
> 'Was it hard to learn?'
>
> 'Not very. You start by going round and round the floor of the pit. That gets you gradually immune to the really terrible giddiness. Then you open up the throttle and the speed takes you on the wall. But once on the wall you find it difficult to come off! You just shut off the throttle ...'
>
> 'How do you keep fit?'
>
> 'I do 30 shows a day!'[6]

Associated Wall of Death events at various dates between the two wars included in Scotland, one New Year, several lads 'First Footed' by visiting Egbert's lion in its cage, without permission or supervision.

In late 1939 the showman Barry had to lay off his thirty-five employees, shoot his lions (including Egbert's lion which he had obviously bought when Egbert returned to America) and close down his wall. He decided to build himself an air-raid shelter out of four walls of death, which was large enough to take twenty people.

Somewhere in the country a motorcyclist (not a Wall of Death rider) was fined for practising Wall of Death tricks – riding side-saddle, standing up, putting his legs over the front – on his motorcycle on the road.

During the mid-1930s some fairgrounds banned walls of death because of a very few deaths, in one case a member of the audience, in another a rider. Some banned them because of the use of lions, or banned walls with animals.

Elias Harris was fined by customs and excise for running out of 6d tickets and selling two 3d tickets instead. His excuse was that he did not have time to go to a city and buy more tickets – he had 300 people waiting to see his wall.

The Xmas/New Year Agricultural Halls in London cancelled the annual event.

By the end of September Bob and Trude sold their share of the wall to my parents, who continued to run the wall for eleven years after the war.

---

1. *The World's Fair,* 4 March 1939.
2. Recorded memories of Jackie Soutter.
3. *The World's Fair,* 1 April 1939.
4. Ibid., 22 April 1939.
5. Ibid., 18 May 1939.
6. *The Littlewood Sports Log* report by Jane Doe, 1939.

18

The War Years

Uncle Frank had fled Italy in 1939. By 1941 he was working for Hawker Bros in Quedgeley but was taken to court for not having a driving licence, which he said he could not afford.

During the war he lived in a caravan with Vivienne and their son on Challings Farm in Abingdon, Oxfordshire, and according to the farmer's son, Dick Deane, they ate every night in the farmhouse. Frank stored his wall and lorries on the farm and became very friendly with the farmer. Bob and Trude Todd also lived there. Frank and Bob eventually both obtained government contracts to haul stone, gravel, etc. to help build wartime airfields near Abingdon.[1]

Uncle Jack, who moved to Stamford, also obtained a government contract and used his lorries by transporting sand and gravel for Pollards in Tallington to local wartime airfields being built.[2]

> Construction of Rutland's second military airfield at Woolfox Lodge began in 1940. Throughout the latter part of that year Stamford was filled with a constant stream of lorries, hauling material from the quarries at Tallington. The lorries would rumble their way down High Street, loaded to the gunnels and streaming water. Needless to say, the streets often had a liberal covering of sand and gravel, at times Red Lion Square resembled a scene from *The Desert Song*. A number of local people bought lorries and went to work transporting material. One of these, a certain Mr Todd, was a 'Wall of Death' rider before his venture into the haulage business.[3]

Uncle Jack also supplied food and equipment to an American air base. He told the story that one day the Base Commander asked Jack to bring something unusual from London for the weekend – it turned out to be a lorry load of women to 'entertain' the troops, contraband whisky and black market food.

Having closed their wall, my parents moved to Wrexham with their caravan and my father also got a government contract to use his lorries to supply gravel etc. to local airports. He also rented a shop and proceeded to fill it with slot machines, pin-ball tables and a little shooting gallery with air rifles and darts. In September 1940 he volunteered at the No. 1 Recruiting Centre in Uxbridge and joined the RAF as an aircraft hand. He was moved around quite a lot to further his skills.

In December 1940 he was sent to the No 11 School of Technical Training at RAF Hereford and later that year he became an Aircraftsman, 2nd Class with very good character. He then trained as a fitter at the School of Technical Training. In 1941 he was sent to 39 Maintenance Unit – he was eventually promoted to Aircraftsman 1st Class and qualified as a special fitter of radial engines. He served until February 1942, when he was released for employment in industry.

George Todd in RAF uniform

His RAF character was V.G., the highest RAF character assessment. He then worked at the Hawker factory in Langley, Slough, on the production line. There were civilian workers at the factory as well and one day my father was called in by the union and told he was working so hard he was showing up all the civilian workers and he was told to slow down. He ignored that and worked even harder!

My parents lived in a caravan on a farm in Banwell, Somerset (where I was born), where they also stored their wall and transport.

From May to December 1944 my father was a member of the Home Guard, and like all others received a certificate of thanks from King George.

In 1942 the government issued a series of posters exhorting the soldiers to fight for Britain, especially traditional Britain. One of the posters, designed by Frank Newbould, shows a very colourful Alfriston Fair, in Sussex. This would seem to support the fact that fairs had become very popular entertainment.

Wyn and George Todd outside their caravan

'Your Britain, Fight for it Now' poster (Crown copyright IWM)

The war had a profound influence on fairgrounds. As Philip Bradley, a great fairground enthusiast, recorded:

> Fairs were affected by blackout restrictions and limited supplies of food, fuel and 'swag'. Coconut shies became rare as coconuts took up valuable shipping space and rifle ranges were deprived of ammunition. Music was also muted in case it drowned out the Alert. Many showmen's engines were used for demolition work clearing debris from blitzed cities and demolishing unstable buildings, especially in areas of severe bomb damage in Merseyside, Manchester and London. Despite these problems some fairs continued, often with blackout protection. Ground previously used for fairs was sometimes turned into allotments to increase productivity, causing travelling fairs to find new sites. Some fairs were held on bombed out areas that had been levelled, whilst others were cancelled altogether due to land being requisitioned for military purposes. Flying-bomb attacks caused nearly all Greater London fairs after mid-June 1944 to be abandoned bringing continued hardship to those families whose livelihood depended on entertaining the crowds. Some larger fairs did take place, such as Nottingham Goose Fair. Special London County Council fairs were also introduced to boost trade, as at Brockwell Park and Tooting Bec Common. ... Another fair was much smaller owing to so many of our members serving in the forces or on work of national importance.[4]

---

1. Letter to the author from Dick Deane, 20 February 1998.
2. Letter to the author from Harry Rowett, 19 February 1998.
3. From *Wings over Rutland* by John Rennison RLHS, 1980, p. 130.
4. From 'Fairgrounds during the Second World War', www.exploringsurreyspast.org.uk, reproduced with kind permission of Surrey Heritage.

Chapter 19

John R. Soutter, My Uncle, Known as Jackie

Born: 1921, Croydon, UK. Married: 1948. Died: 2001 in Australia.
Riding name: Jack Soutter. Rode: 1946–1953.

Whilst my mother and aunt were riding in various seaside resorts in the early 1930s my grandmother rented a house near them during the summer and took all her younger children with her, Jackie, Keith, and Norman – so from a very early age the younger children were aware of the Wall of Death and there are plenty of family photos of them sitting on motorbikes with either of their two sisters, but not on a wall. Also staying in the rented house were the other Wall of Death riders.

Three Soutter boys on bike, 1930s

Early in the 1930s when my mother was riding in Scotland for Codona's Wall of Death in Dundee she invited her younger brother, Jackie, aged 11, to spend the holidays with her. He travelled up to Scotland on his own from his parents' house in Bromley. When he arrived, after a full day's journey, he was met by my mother and Speedy Brum in Speedy's open-top sports car. Jackie asked to go on the wall and he found himself as a pillion rider sitting on a cushion on the tank of Speedy Brum's bike that same evening. The spieler announced that he was the youngest person ever to ride the wall. And he did, twice. Jackie absolutely hated it; he was dizzy, felt sick afterwards and vowed he would never become a rider. A bright side was that the local Scottish lads, whose accent he could not understand, treated him like a hero. Whilst he was still at school he often spent the holidays with my mother.

At fourteen he left school and trained as a chef. When the war started he volunteered for the RAF and spent five years in India.

In 1946 when he left the RAF he went to Ramsgate, where my mother and father had their wall. My father suggested that Jackie learned to roller skate on the wall, so he had special boots made. My father made a gantry at the back of his bike, and he started to learn, attached to a rope in case he fell off. However, they soon came across a problem. Because the wall had been stored during the war, the banking had become damp and rotten, although the upright panels were in good condition. You had to get a government licence to buy as little as 6' of good wood so the banking could not be repaired. A motorbike could run over the small rotten parts but not roller skates. So my father suggested that he taught Jackie to ride a motorcycle instead. Jackie was twenty-four and by the end of the year he was riding and doing tricks on the wall.

For eight years Uncle Jackie rode for my parents and when they were on holiday or working out of the country Jackie took charge of their wall. His memories are very detailed but he did not record them until I asked him to – he was in Australia by then, aged 75, and, as he himself said, he was not sure he always got the dates correct. He did, however, list the towns he recalled that my parents went to with their wall – there are sixty of them, and of course, most of them were visited every year.

He also filled out a questionnaire that I sent him. He listed my father's tricks and considered him the best trick rider in the UK. I quote his comments to the question 'Please describe George's tricks. Was he considered a good trick rider?'

> The best trick rider. Standing on footrests, standing on footrests both feet to one side of the bike then the other. Sitting half side-saddle on either side of bike, while wobbling

> the bike with his foot and backside pressure and zigzagging up and down the wall. Sitting full side-saddle on both sides and eventually facing completely backwards (most difficult and dangerous), left foot on handlebars, right foot on handlebars, both feet on handlebars. Sitting completely on handlebars, one foot on footrest and one on front forks. Most tricks done with hands in the air, while zigzagging up and down the wall.[1]

As far as my mother was concerned:

> The best female trick rider. Standing up, sitting half saddle. One foot on handlebars. Both feet on handlebars. Sitting on petrol tank. Sitting on handlebars. All above with hands off handlebars and zigzagging from top to bottom of the wall.

Jackie himself did tricks similar to George, although he did not consider himself a good trick rider. He did once, however, ride blindfolded.

In 1949, when my parents were riding in Switzerland, Jackie ran their wall. My father had employed two riders, Joyce and Jo Franklin. Jo could not trick ride and Joyce only did straight rides. According to my uncle they wore their riding breeches and riding boots all the time, even when not on the wall. Jo thought it was good publicity and he was proud to be a rider. They even wore them walking down Piccadilly and enjoyed people turning round and saying 'there go a couple of Wall of Death riders'. However, in Southsea Jo had an accident on the wall and broke his arm, crashing into Jackie's bike on the way down. Shell-Mex filmed them in Southsea and you can see the Hell Drivers' Race, Uncle Jackie on the bally and Jo and Joyce Franklin.[2]

Jackie also booked a fair in Wisborough Green, Sussex. He said:

> The fair was for about a week but you didn't book any ground, you didn't pay to go on but you lined up with your trucks and trailers on Sunday outside on the road and at 12 noon you were allowed into the park to build up. At 12 noon there was a great rush of showmen to get in, trying to get the best position.

Jackie had had 2,000 flyers printed advertising 'George Todd's Hell Drivers – a show not to be missed' and distributed them twenty miles around the area, throwing them into the street or handing them to small boys. He saw an AA man picking up leaflets and then pinning them to telegraph poles. The other showmen had seen the leaflets and at 12 noon were waiting for Jackie to choose a position for the wall before all jostling to get a position near it. It caused chaos, the council was called, and the mayor arrived and asked Jackie to move his wall. Totally out of the question because it took about six hours to put up a wall. However, when they opened at 6 o'clock there was a huge queue, 99 per cent of whom were the other showmen. During the whole fair he had so many customers he had to run twice as many shows per hour. Eventually the mayor returned and asked to use the microphone. He did, said it was a wonderful show, the most thrilling thing he had seen in his life, a top-class performance, and he recommended everyone listening to go and tell their relatives to come to the Wall of Death.[3]

Incidentally most of the showmen were old travellers who had had no schooling and could not read or write. Many of them kept going to my uncle to get him to read their letters from councils, contractors etc. so Jackie became quite popular.

At one fair near Hastings on Bonfire Night, hooligans began throwing fireworks into the people watching the demonstrations on the bally. Jackie got quite scared and threatened to call the police, but the hooligans just got worse. Eventually the other showmen rallied round, big hefty fellows some of them, and the hooligans soon dispersed.

At a fair in Sheffield one New Year my father employed a rider called George Hendry, known as Speedy Hendry. Jackie was in charge of the wall. Hendry decided to ride the wall with the door to the bally open (something never done), without telling Jackie. Hendry hit the door, smashed up his bike and was taken to hospital with a police escort. So Jackie had to send a telegram to my father: 'Todd, Smugglers Barn. Hendry crashed – in hospital with broken arm. Can you come and ride. Signed Wall of Death'. The girl in the post office thought the telegram very gruesome.

At Wisbech Jackie was riding a bike on the rollers on the high bally doing tricks and a good crowd were watching. Suddenly the rollers jammed and he shot off the bally like a rocket towards the crowd below. The crowd scattered so no-one except Jackie was hurt. He broke his wrist, but rode again that same evening. Thereafter, however, he could not ride for six weeks because he was in so much pain.

In 1949–50 the wall was at Olympia over Christmas and New Year. In January Prince Michael, aged 7, and his older brother the Duke of Kent were taken to see the performance. When Jackie asked them if they wanted a ride Prince Michael said yes but his accompanying officials would not let him. The photos of the two royals watching Jackie trick riding were in many national newspapers, including the Daily Graphic, captioned 'Look no hands ... and seven-year-old Prince Michael held his breath as the rider on the Wall of Death at Olympia roared "round and round" till the Prince took up the idea'.[4]

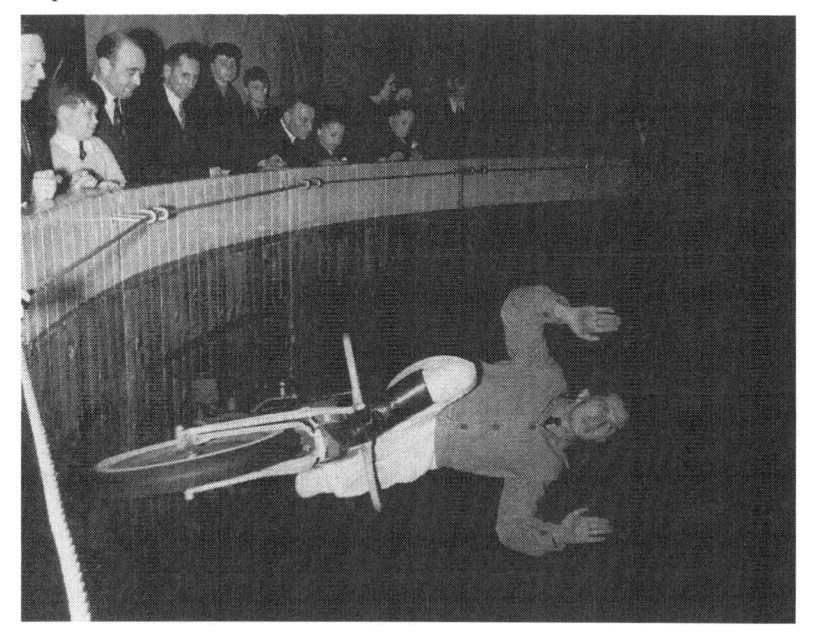

Jackie Soutter rides before Prince Michael and the Duke of Kent, 1950

Also at Olympia Billy Butlin turned up one evening, very late and very drunk, demanding to be allowed to ride the wall. Eventually, after much argument, Jackie allowed him to do so. He had no idea how to ride and very soon crashed and broke his arm.

In 1951 Jackie stopped travelling with my parents and bought a greengrocer's shop in Ramsgate, but did ride on their wall in Dreamland, Margate, until 1953, when he eventually gave up. In 1962 he and his family emigrated to Australia, but he did not ride there.

---

1. Jackie Soutter's recorded memories.
2. See Shell-Mex film in Southsea on http://www.youtube.com/watch?v=oK9T72tBiFE.
3. Jackie Soutter's recorded memories.
4. *Daily Graphic*, 12 January 1950.

Chapter 20

Wyn and George Todd after the Second World War

Fairs and amusement parks started to re-open in the spring of 1945. There were probably only about twelve walls operating in the UK after the Second World War, including three belonging to the Todd family. A few weeks after the end of the war my parents were asked to take their wall to Clarence Pier Amusement Park in Southsea, Hampshire. The amusement park was run by the showman Billy Manning, so the wall was under his name. My parents were very friendly with the Manning family, most of whom were showmen and members of the Showmen's Guild. In 1946 Billy and another showman, Georgie Peak, wrote a joke letter to my parents, asking to be employed as riders although neither of them rode the wall and they were not in prison either.

Clarence Pier, Southsea, 1948

OLYMPIA, EARLSCOURT, N.7.
Nr. Wormwood Scrubs.
18th July, 1946.

Dear George, Madam Win,

Here we are , two first class straight and trick acrobatic riders, complete with lady. We will be willing to ride for you until the end of September providing we can have 75% of gross takings, and 100% of Drop.

We are willing to start immediately, but you must guarantee us work at Olympia, Royal Agricultural Hall, Kelvin Hall, Glasgow, with the option of touring Kings Lynn, Wiesbeach, Stanford, Grantham, and guarantee us a most successful Easter, on Wanstead Flats. If a wet Easter, one Weekend on the Wheel-in, at March Cambridgeshire, without drop.

Should the above proposals not meet with your approval, we shall have to offer our services to Sir Frederick Lee, Sir William Thomas Long, for the season at Barry.

Yours faithfully,
Two Boys that really Mean Business

Billy Manning
George Peel

Joke letter to my parents

As my mother recorded in her diary in 1945:

> The wall, the lorries and the bikes were unearthed from sheds and farmers' fields and taken to Southsea and the effort of getting it built up again began. Before it was finished and before any of us had ridden it again a queue had formed at the entrance right to the end of the amusement park. George got the bikes running and we let the people in. The tyres were rotten, and we had not been on the wall for all the war years. That old saying 'the show must go on' is something very true in the minds of all show people and it is just a natural instinct and we put on the show and carried on. Three times during the first week our tyres went flat whilst we were riding, but with what can only have been sheer good luck we managed to make the floor in an upright position. We had not expected

> business to be very good after the war but it was. The wood on the banking – the starting track onto the wall – had rotted slightly but this did not stop the bikes from riding round it and up onto the wall.[1]

They worked on the amusement parks in the summer, travelled the fairs in the spring and autumn and went to Olympia for Christmas and New Year. They travelled a lot with Billy Smart's Circus but at Olympia it was in conjunction with Billy Smart and Bertram Mills' Circus. Since they owned their wall until 1956 it was not always possible for me to decide when and what dates they were at which fairs or amusements parks.

Early in 1946 my father advertised in *The World's Fair* for riders and a spieler for four months at the seaside. This was at Ramsgate, Thanet, Kent at the Merrie England amusement park.

Merrie England, Ramsgate

In June the same year my father put a very large advertisement in the paper and offered £15 a week to riders, plus a percentage of the nobbins (the tips thrown down after each performance) to appear at Merrie England and then at fairs in the autumn, after the summer season finished. That was a very good rate of pay at that time. I never found any other advertisement which advertised pay for riders.[2]

In November 1946 he again advertised for a trick rider. They stayed at Merrie England in 1947, '48 and '49, still travelling the fairs before and after the summer season. In 1946 they had bought a property in Pegwell Bay, Thanet, Kent. This was, in fact, several sixteenth-century flint cottages and a barn, which had been condemned by the local council as unfit for habitation. However, my father clearly persuaded the council that he could restore the properties and he did so.

Over Christmas and New Year 1946–47 they appeared at Olympia, London, over a four-week period. Then in March 1947 they were at Wisbech and March and my father again advertised in *The World's Fair* for riders and a spieler.[3] They spent the 1947 summer at Merrie England, Ramsgate, Kent.

My uncle Jackie Soutter also recalled at Ramsgate:

> George also rigged up a waxworks. He got hold of some old figures from somewhere, old heads and a big box of all sorts of bits and pieces. He had a pitch inside Merrie England where he could put up a wall and a length of curtain and he made a sideshow, called The Chamber of Horrors. We tried to get all the information we could about bad people – there was an opium den and Blue Beard's murder in the bath but I don't recall whose faces we had. Probably Nelson doing the murder of some film star being killed with a saw or something but we made various settings and tableaux of these horrific deeds of the past. My brother Keith and I also rigged up some nylon thread and fixed it to the heads of various figures and from the cash box we could see a little way in and we had these cords in the cash box, quite invisible to paying visitors, and as people would go in the first tableau was an opium den with a fierce looking Chinese man sitting there. We waited until a family of boys and girls were looking at it and then walking away and invariably one or a couple of them would look back and we'd pull the string and move the Chinese man's head. Well there were screams and they'd say 'looks as though he moved his head'. They would then run along the corridor and my brother and I had this massive giant mask, which we kept in a cupboard half way through the waxworks, and we'd come out of this cupboard with this head on to scare people. We had some fun with that. The elderly ladies who came down from London thought it was the best money's worth they had ever spent.[4]

In 1948 they started the season at Stamford for a week. Again my father advertised for a spieler and driver in *The World's Fair*.[5] I remember Stamford very well because the river flooded and went all over the fairground. H. M. Rowett recalled 'the river rose dramatically and flooded the whole of Bath Row and was creeping up Castle Dyke towards Jo Ling's Ben Hur Ride' (a fairground attraction). At the age of 80 Mr Rowett also wrote 'I remember the Hell Drivers on the car park'.[6]

It is quite clear that owners, including my father and his brothers, were frequently advertising for riders. I think my father constantly wanted new riders because he would only accept the very best riders and those who did not constantly come up to his high expectations did not have their contracts renewed. There was an added problem in that riders, once trained, would often go and ride for someone else.

By April 1948 they were in Clapham Common and then in Epping, where it was reported in *The World's Fair* that 'George Todd and his Hell Drivers, not forgetting Wyn Soutter, who is a very daring rider' were appearing.[7]

That year, after appearing at Tottenham Fair for three weeks, which closed late Saturday evening, they were booked to appear at Chichester for the following Monday only. By the time they had pulled down in Tottenham it was 2 a.m. They had to drive through the night to get to Chichester. According to Uncle Jackie Soutter my father bought some bicycle lamps – two for the front of each truck and a red one at the back of each. After stopping for a break they discovered the lamps had dropped off! Later that year my father bought a new Ford lorry, a second-hand Ford and a big Ford trailer, but even these did not have trailer brakes.

In January 1949, my father again advertised for a lady or gent rider and a spieler/driver from March until Christmas.[8] They employed Johnny Dare, whom they taught to ride, and who stayed with them until the four-week Olympia booking finished. In the autumn of 1949 my parents also rode a wall in Switzerland (covered in Chapter 23.)

Whitsun 1950 saw the first coupon-free petrol available since 1939, which meant car owners could go on more outings. In 1950 my parents returned to Clarence Pier in Southsea for the summer season, toured in the spring and autumn and appeared at Olympia over the Christmas period 1950–51. By this time I was 9 years old and during

Wyn Todd on rollers, 1950s

the summer stayed with them on Clarence Pier. We had a caravan parked behind the wall and I remember going to sleep to the noise of the motorbikes. We had a dog called Pimms, who 'guarded' me in the caravan when I was alone. Showmen's children got free rides on all the rides and I spent a considerable time on them, thoroughly enjoying myself.

Author at Clarence Pier, Southsea

The Hell Drivers, 1950, George and Wyn Todd, Jackie Soutter and Paddy

In the spring and autumn they appeared, amongst other towns, at Hastings, Tunbridge Wells and Tonbridge, when *The World's Fair* reported that George Todd and Jack Soutter presented the Race of Death and Winifred Soutter was billed as England's first and foremost lady wall rider.[9]

For the summer season 1951 they appeared at Dreamland, Margate, and my father again advertised in *The World's Fair* for riders for Dreamland and fairs until Christmas.[10] Thereafter they stayed at Dreamland until late 1955. It was very near to our Pegwell Bay home and therefore very convenient for the summer booking.

Dreamland, Margate, 1950s

George Todd trick riding

Apart from my uncle, Jackie Soutter, my parents also trained other riders. These included Johnny Dare, Joe Barker, Freddie Lee and Keith Bonner. They also employed an Irish man called Paddy, who did not ride but helped out driving, selling tickets, erecting and pulling down the wall and looking after me from time to time. My father told the Wall of Death owner, Allan Ford , his experience with teaching Freddie Lee, who, at first, could not get the bike further up the wall than the banking. My father got some of Freddie's girlfriends to come and watch and egg him on. Freddie responded by riding to the safety cable and then over the top and out of the wall altogether, although he was totally unhurt.

One year they appeared at Guy Fawkes Celebrations at Edenbridge, Kent, then the biggest bonfire celebration in the country. There had never been a fair there before but my father went to see the organizers and they agreed to let him run a small fair. They were ready to open the wall in the afternoon but nobody came and by two minutes to eight there was still nobody. After eight, when the town processions had finished, hundreds if not thousands of people trooped into the fair. It was bedlam – they were trying to get up the entry steps of the wall with their flaming torches. My mother was in the pay box and terrified. The pay box was not very strong, and together with the flaming torches she thought the whole show would be burnt. There were people shouting 'Burn them down, Burn them down'.

One member of the audience had a heart attack whilst watching the show and had to be lowered down on the outside of the wall because of the crowds. Just before 10 p.m. the fairground emptied, people rushing to get the last trains home. My parents had taken a record amount of money in just two hours – a record never broken.

They once appeared at Christmas at Kennard's department store in Croydon in their large basement. I remember it well because the whole store was decorated with huge trees and decorations.

They also appeared at Horsham, Sussex.

Early in 1951, whilst appearing at Olympia, the BBC made a radio recording, which was broadcast afterwards. Alan Dixon was the reporter, using very early

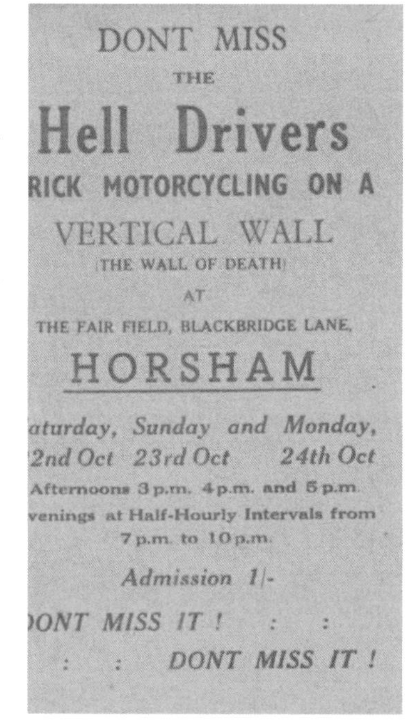

Hell Drivers flyer, Horsham

and very large portable recording equipment. It was the first time such equipment had been used for an outside broadcast. My father carried the equipment on his back and Alan Dixon sat in front of him on the bike and was not only quite scared but was also leaning the wrong way, making it difficult for my father to steer properly. After the ride, once Alan Dixon had recovered, he interviewed my mother and father and my uncle Jackie Soutter. In this interview my father stated that he had been riding the wall since 1929 and my uncle said how interesting riding the wall was and that they had been seen by many famous people, including royalty. The recording equipment had been somewhat damaged and my mother sounded like Mickey Mouse when she spoke. My father paid a company to record the episode onto a vinyl disc, which I still own. The British Sound Archive, based at the British Library, has now transferred this disc onto a CD.

Another year at Olympia over Christmas the Shell Oil Company from Shell-Mex House in London asked if they could make a film of the show. As my uncle Jackie Soutter remembered:

> One day we had a visit from several high-ranking representatives from the Shell Oil Company, from Shell-Mex House in London. They said they had a professional film crew, who were making interesting films, mainly about motor cars, motorbikes and the petroleum and oil trade, and they'd like to make a film of our Wall of Death. Of course George [my father] said yes and they turned up with a full film crew, with cameras and lights, clip board men, continuity girl, script checkers or writers, a whole caboodle of them, very professional, and also, of course, a director. We spent several days during the quiet period, mainly when the circus wasn't performing, when there weren't many people about. We went in early some mornings and they made quite a good film. At one stage George had a camera strapped to the back of his motorbike and he went up on the wall and I rode behind him and did a series of tricks a few feet from his back wheel. Now whilst we made certain calculations to allow for the curve of the wall, and lifted the camera up so that it would take my picture, we didn't allow for the pressure that you get riding the Wall of Death, pushing not only the bike, because we had no springs on the bike, but mainly the camera was being forced down, the same as when you take a pillion passenger for a ride on your tank, they get forced down and you have to hold their heads back. Apparently the camera got forced down. This we didn't realize until the film was processed

> and printed and we'd stopped making the film. So instead of a film of me doing tricks on the bike, all they got was a film of my wheel. I must say it was very effective, they used it when they edited and made the film, up, to good advantage, flashed onto it for a second and there was this wheel and you could see the boards of the wall flying underneath, you could almost see the angle it was going – gave quite an impression of high speed but unfortunately not a frontal close up of the tricks. Anyway the film was duly made, the Shell-Mex film company were quite generous, and anyway it would have been generous in those days in their gratuities and payments to us all and payments to George for his expenses. This was Xmas 1949 through January 1950. We finished our season at Olympia and all packed up and went home. George and Wyn went to Switzerland for a ski holiday and while they were away we heard from Shell-Mex with an invitation. Gladys [his wife] and I went up to London at the invitation of the film director of the Shell-Mex unit and we had a private viewing in Shell-Mex's own private theatre. It was very good, very professionally done, after which we were taken to Soho for a scrumptious lunch – boy that film director knew how to eat – oysters and champagne, you name it and we had it, and Gladys and I had a good time. Well no more was heard of the film, I forget what the name was. Apparently it was good enough to find itself into the film library of the BBC TV service, which likely they used when things had finished early and they had five or ten minutes or a quarter of an hour to fill in between programmes. Well lo and behold, they showed our film one day or evening – none of us saw it but, of course, George heard about it and got very annoyed, well he pretended to be annoyed anyway. I think he thought he was going to make some money out of it. He complained bitterly to the BBC that they had no right to show the film with him performing, it was his show and a picture of George Todd's Hell Drivers, and that he should be paid for it. He employed a solicitor, I think, to write to them. I've got a feeling George did get some money for the first showing on TV, I don't think it was very much – he also got the promise that the film would be taken out of the library and never used again. And that's the last we ever saw or heard of that film and our starring in the movies.'[11]

In 1951 the BBC Northern Children's Hour broadcast a programme *Living with Thrills* featuring my parents' wall.

The lorries that my parents owned were quite old, with wooden driving cabs, holes in the floor so you could see the roads below and lights that did not really work properly. They also had trailers and a big old Dennis, the engine of which used to drive the generators to give light to the wall when built up. One of the trailers was used as the bally in front of the built-up wall. The trailers had no brakes, which was illegal but not uncommon at the time. Lorries had to be started with a starting handle.

One of the riders my parents trained was Keith Bonner, who rode for them between 1951 and 1954. He rode at Dreamland, Margate, but also travelled the fairs. He recalled it cost one shilling to go in but when the crowds were sparse it was reduced to sixpence. They appeared, amongst other places he remembered, at King's Lynn in March. Dreamland opened from Whitsun to the end of September. They toured with only one lorry and a large trailer. Keith remembered two of the six bikes, a 1922 and a 1928 Indian Scout. He recalled appearing at Nottingham Goose Fair, Hull, where they appeared under the showmen Marshall Bros. And Marshall took 50 per cent of my parents' takings ... The busiest days were weekends and Bank Holidays, at which time they rode six shows an hour for ten hours a day. As with all riders who did not have a caravan Keith thought the worst thing about travelling was finding digs, which invariably had no baths. Meals were a problem too, eating in cafes where they could only get fried food.

Keith considered my father to be the best trick rider in Britain (as others did) and he described my father's tricks as follows:

> The ones I saw him do were sitting either side of the machine in different attitudes, sitting on the machine and then turning to face the rear; standing with the left foot on the board and the right foot on the spring at the same time as dipping up and down the wall. A trick that none of us were happy with, standing under the machine facing upwards. (I used to droop over it like a wet cabbage and I gave that one up in the end.)

Keith always found building up and pulling down the wall more painful than riding. He concluded:

> Certainly my days on the Wall of Death are amongst the happiest memories I have – being single which contributed to it. It's a very carefree existence and being stationary at seaside resorts I had a great deal of free time to spare; spent a great deal of time swimming. The attention of many girls was highly desirable.[12]

I think the last sentence was one of the reasons young men applied to learn to ride. Wall riders, especially in the 1930s, were treated somewhat like celebrities and perhaps even more so in the 1950s, when there were fewer around. Once Keith left my father's wall he went on to ride for my uncle, Frank Todd Senior.

In 1955 Louis Shwarootz (Curly Lou Cody), my mother's riding partner in 1930 including at the Munich Oktoberfest, stopped over at London Airport and contacted the press. He was trying to find my mother. He spent several hours telephoning people in order to find her. It was reported in several papers and headed 'Death Rider in search of a sweetheart'. Louis stated that twenty-four years ago my mother had been his girlfriend, as well as his riding partner. Although it was also reported in my mother's local paper she was on holiday. Her sister Gladys, however, read the reports and contacted Louis. He was still riding a Wall of Death and he wanted to ride again with my mother. According to the reports Louis went to Ramsgate to meet my mother and aunt – but my mother had given up riding so declined his offer to team up again.[13]

Also in 1955 my father's wall was used in a political cartoon. Labour had lost the General Election and Harold Wilson, Shadow Chancellor, chaired an internal Labour Party enquiry into the organization. Highly critical of the organization, Wilson referred to it as a 'Penny Farthing Machine in a jet age'. A week later the report was discussed at the Labour Party Annual Conference held in Margate, Kent. The cartoon depicts Dreamland Amusement Park and its variety of attractions, including my parents' Wall of Death. Wilson is seen leaning against the wall with a penny farthing bike and the words 'Hurtling Harold and his NEW Machine' and 'Stupendous Attraction'. All the other characters in the cartoons are various members of the Labour Party.[14]

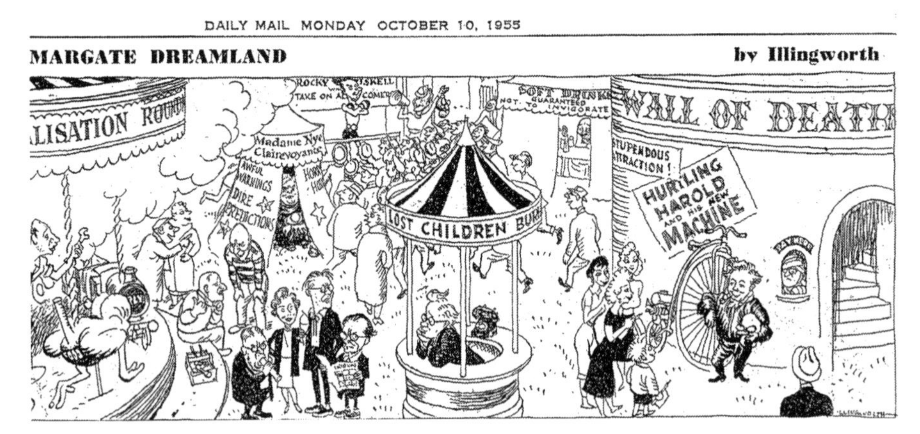

Harold Wilson cartoon, Dreamland, 1955 (copyright *Daily Mail*)

In January 1956, my father advertised their wall for sale in *The World's Fair.*[15] He was selling the wall, two trailers, six Indian motorbikes and spares, all in good condition. After two more advertisements he sold the wall to Peter Catchpole, a rider, for £250. My father was a very astute businessman and he predicted that fairs and amusement parks would gradually go into decline and it would be difficult to make money.

So ended my parents' careers on the Wall of Death. They then opened an antique business in Pegwell Bay, Thanet, Kent, together with a restaurant on the premises. My father taught himself to restore antique furniture, jewellery and other items, and to make furniture and restore antique garden ornaments – many bought from demolished buildings and cinemas – and sold them. The display of the ornaments on the large forecourt was often shown in the local papers and generated considerable local interest. They ran the antique business until their deaths.

When I was a teenager I decided I wanted to become a Wall of Death rider – after all I had been surrounded by owners and riders all my life. My mother objected, saying I was too young, and it was only years after that I realized she had been a famous rider at the early age of 15!

---

1. Wyn Todd's 1945 diary.
2. *The World's Fair,* June 1946.
3. Ibid., March 1947.
4. Jackie Soutter's recorded memories.
5. *The World's Fair,* February 1948.
6. Letter to author from H. M. Rowett, 8 January 1999.
7. *The World's Fair,* April 1948.
8. Ibid., January 1949.
9. Ibid., October 1950.
10. Ibid., August 1951.
11. Jackie Soutter's recorded memories.
12. Keith Bonner's memories told to Allan Ford, 1999, with Allan's kind permission.
13. *Daily Sketch,* 16 March 1955.
14. *Daily Mail,* 10 October 1955.
15. *The World's Fair,* January 1956.

Chapter 21
Franco Todd, My Cousin – Known as Frankie

Born: Genoa, Italy, 1932. Married: 1957. Died: 1981 in Spain.
Rode: 1951–late 1960s.

Frankie's parents were both Wall of Death riders/owners: Miss Vivienne and his father, Frank Todd Senior. Frankie was brought up in Italy until he was seven with his parents who had their Wall of Death there from 1932 to 1939. His father maintained a very comprehensive photograph album of their time in Italy, which contains many unpublished Wall of Death photographs from there.

Frankie started riding at the Festival of Britain Amusement Park in 1951 aged 19, on his father's wall. At the Festival Frankie had an accident riding and was taken to hospital for observation. He also rode for his father on the Silodrome at the Battersea Park Funfair in 1953.

In 1953 Frankie appeared at the Munich Oktoberfest on Kitty Muller's wall, one of four international riders, an Austrian, an Italian, a German and Frankie. I went there with my parents to see him ride. I had my photograph taken with the four riders and also a photo of the wall itself, known as Kitty and Pitt's wall.

Their photographs and reports were in the German local newspapers. A photo of the four was also printed on the front page of *The World's Fair*, who also printed a long letter he wrote to them giving his impressions of the Oktoberfest: 'The business this year more than came up to everyone's expectations, the middle Sunday of the three weekends bringing in what was estimated to be well over half a million people.' He also described new rides, including the 'Figure of Eight – the sensation of the Oktoberfest this year', and he was very impressed with the lighting of the whole fair – he considered German showmen led the world in this respect. He also reported on the ten big beer halls, each seating between six and nine thousand people, whilst the whole ox roasting on a spit over a charcoal fire was a 'sight for sore eyes for any visiting Englishman'.[1]

Kitty and Pitt Wall of Death, Oktoberfest, 1953

Author with Pitt, Frankie, Kitty and Mia

Frankie on the rollers

Pitt, Mia, Kitty and Frankie

Frankie clearly stayed in Germany with his own wall for in July he advertised in *The World's Fair* for a lady rider from then until December.

By 1954 his father had retired but Frankie continued to tour the UK and appeared in Dundee in June and *The World's Fair* had a photo of him with Yvonne Stagg on the front of his bike. It seems that the riders were called The Three Brooklands, which included Britain's youngest rider (Stagg), but those claims about age were not always correct.

By 1955 Frankie had his wall at Barry Island, Wales, for the summer season and in May advertised that he wanted to train a Welsh girl to appear at Barry Island and go on a sixteen-day Continental tour. Frankie also rode a go-cart on the wall.[2]

Frankie on go-cart

Frankie trick riding

He was successful in this appeal. He then permanently stayed at Barry Island for the summer season, presumably touring before and after the season. One of the riders he employed was Horace Parker, with whom he performed the Race of Death. When Horace Parker and his brother Len owned their own wall some time after, Len was killed when erecting the wall when one of the panels fell on him and crushed him. There were very few Wall of Death fatalities, despite all the warnings in the 1930s that it was a dangerous act.

Frankie Todd and Horace Parker in Race of Death

By about 1970 Frankie had given up his wall and opened a pub on Barry Island, Cardiff. Years later he went to live in Spain, where he died of a heart attack in 1981, six weeks before his father's death.

He was the last of my family to ride and own a wall.

---

1. *The World's Fair,* 31 October 1953.
2. Ibid., 15 May 1955.

Chapter 22
Frank Todd Senior after the Second World War

Uncle Bob and Uncle Jack gave up the wall after the war and both became antique dealers. Frank Todd Senior continued with his wall and in 1945 took his wall to Barry Island, Wales, from where he advertised for riders.[1] Again in November he advertised for male and female riders for a five-week Christmas booking somewhere. He stayed at Barry Island in 1946, calling himself Frank Todd's Atomic Riders.

In 1947 for the summer season he appeared at Clarence Pier in Southsea, advertising for a lady rider or pillion rider in May.[2] As usual for Clarence Pier this was a Billy Manning concession and the photo shows this clearly. After the summer season he toured and appeared at Tewkesbury Mop.[3]

Frank Todd's wall, Clarence Pier, Southsea, 1947

He again spent the 1948 summer season at Southsea and he advertised for riders in February and December. At this time he was still living on the farm that he lived on during the war. In 1949 he returned to Clarence Pier, Southsea, for the summer, again advertising for riders. In October he appeared at Abingdon's Michaelmas Fair: 'Visitors inspected the stalls and side-shows. Many stood gazing up at the chief attraction the "Wall of Death" in the market place.' The wall was called Todd's Wall. Fifty years later this short piece was re-printed in the paper under their '50 years ago' column.[4]

In September he was at Glastonbury, again advertising for riders.[5]

In 1950 Frank spent the summer season at Southport Pleasureland.

Johnnie Bates, a rider, once said that Frank was the 'best rider he ever saw for his flair and showmanship and also in his car on the wall he would be rubbing the [safety] cable for a show in Southport'. Later in the year Frank had his wall under Albert Evans' name in Scotland, where he was still driving his adapted Austin 7. He had also contracted to ride for Evans in 1951 but he failed to turn up – he had had a better offer to appear at The Festival of Britain in London. Albert Evans sued for breach of contract and won £900 damages, which, according to his son, my uncle never paid.

The Festival of Britain was firstly to celebrate the 100th anniversary of the 1851 Great Exhibition. Secondly it was to be a boost to the nation after the Second World War:

> The Festival of Britain provided the government with an unprecedented opportunity to further the cause of modern British design. ... it caught the public imagination. 10,000,000 visited the London South Bank site ... the BBC broadcast over 2,700 programmes on themes.[6]

It was on a twenty-seven-acre site and opened by the King. The fair was called The Festival Pleasure Gardens, also known as Battersea Fun Fair. The guide to the fair included a pull-out graphic illustration, which, unfortunately, was produced well before the gardens opened and there is no mention of the Wall of Death.

The *Illustrated London News* commissioned illustrations, one of which was by Bryan de Grineau in which he illustrated the gardens and included the Wall of Death at the bottom right corner. Frank's wall was called 'The Wall of Death, Hell Drivers'.

He took over £20,000 during the festival – a considerable amount of money in those days. Horace Parker and Frankie Todd junior also rode with him and they trained a young woman, Yvonne Stagg. I was ten at the time and still remember going to see my uncle and cousin on their wall. Parker had a crash and was taken to hospital. Because the amusement park was so popular it continued in 1952 and 1953 at Battersea, with Frank's wall. He renamed it the Silodrome. Frankie still rode for him as did Keith Bonner, whom my father had trained at Dreamland. Battersea Fair closed in October 1953. The price to enter the pleasure garden was 6d.

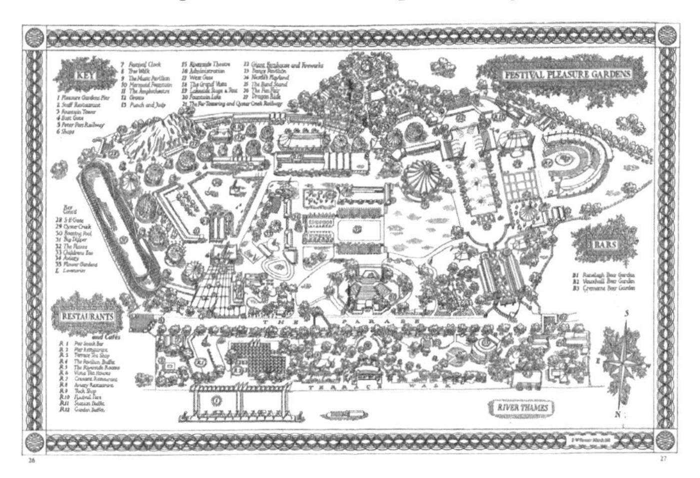

Festival Pleasure Gardens (copyright RIBA)

Festival Pleasure Gardens sketch (copyright Museum of London)

Although Uncle Jack Todd did not have his wall there he did have several shows and had bought Sir Malcolm Campbell's Blue Bird car, which he exhibited.

In late 1952 and early 1953 Frank toured Yorkshire and Scotland but he eventually retired in 1953, with a notice in *The World's Fair* to this effect.

Frank Todd's wall, Festival Pleasure Gardens, 1951

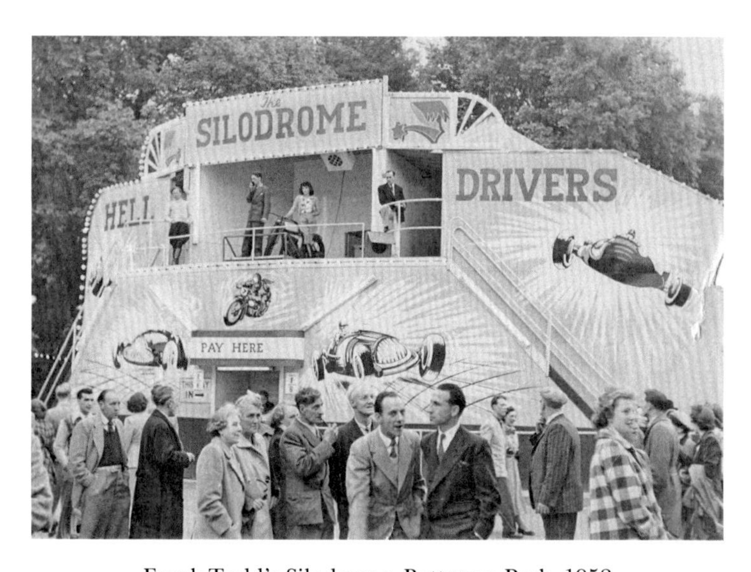

Frank Todd's Silodrome, Battersea Park, 1952

In July 1953, *The World's Fair* printed a very long article about him, together with a photograph of him driving one of his cars on the wall. The article, by The Pertinent Penman, but clearly taken after interviewing Frank, concluded:

> During his time Frank Todd introduced novelties on to the wall; for instance roller skating as actually performed by his

> brother Robert. Frank it was who put two cars on the wall and had lions as passengers. When in Abyssinia he found that the locals prayed for him as he took the lions round on the wall.[7]

I have never seen a photo of Frank with his lions.

When he retired he became an antique dealer in a large property in Uckfield, Sussex. I visited his home many times with my parents and then with my husband and children. He also sold very high-quality imported Italian reproduction furniture.

He had quite a list of celebrity clients, including Princess Margaret. By this time Miss Vivienne, his wife, was no longer on the scene and his partner was Elizabeth. Frank was driving his car with Elizabeth as the passenger when he had a very nasty crash and Elizabeth was killed. He never recovered from this tragedy and moved away from Uckfield to London, where he opened another antique shop. He suffered yet another tragedy when his son, Frankie, died six weeks before he himself died.

Frank's Indian motorbike has been restored and is being ridden by Danny Varrenne Junior in France, having previously been owned and ridden by Benito Manfredini (Italian), Roland Janneret (Swiss) and Daniel Varenne Senior (French), so it has been around!

Frank Todd's Indian, 2016 (copyright Danny Varrane)

---

1. *The World's Fair*, June 1945.
2. Ibid., May 1947.
3. Ibid., 11 November 1947.
4. *North Berks Herald and Didcot Advertiser*, October 1949 and 1999.
5. *The World's Fair*, 10 September 1941.
6. Professor J. Woodham, *The Industrial Designer and the Public.* London: Pembridge History of Design Series, 1983.
7. *The World's Fair*, 25 May 1953.

Chapter 23

Wyn and George on the Swiss Wall, 1949

My parents have been going skiing in Switzerland since 1936. I have come to the conclusion that during one of their many trips by car they saw a Swiss Wall of Death owned by Paula Zeigen and her husband Hans and that after the war Paula contacted them to ask them to ride for her. So in 1949 that is what they did, leaving their own wall in charge of my mother's brother, Jackie Soutter.

My mother kept a diary of the trip as follows:

5th Sep 1949

Arrived Ostend about 8 in the evening. Fixed a room for the night. Had dinner, no good, walked round town, had coffee, went to bed.

6th. Had to change English money to pay the bill. Road to Brussels started good turned very bad, stopped in Brussels for coffee.

Bought rolls, ham and pastries and beer and had picnic lunch on road. Better country than France, good road. Got to Luxembourg about 6. Big fair in the town, was surprised to see Tom Arnold's Ice Revue as the star show in a travelling booth. Had dinner – good – and carried on into France, arrived Metz about 10 pm. Fixed room for the night, Metropole, opposite La Gare – morbid – couldn't sleep much for trains.

7th. Got going about 9.30. Stopped for lunch at Epinal, good, clean and cheerful. Got to Mulhouse about 4.30 and had some tea. Made Basle about 6 and carried on to Zurich. Felt tired by the time we arrived, found our way quite easily to Albisgutli [sic] and found Paula Zeigen in the caravan. Very much like an English fair, the wall looks like a toy. They have fixed up a small room for us across the road in the attic of a restaurant, only a small single bed, but comforting to have somewhere to sleep.

Don't like the thought of that little wall, it is only 24 foot across. Paula cooked us three eggs each and we went to bed.

Paula Zeigen's wall – George Todd centre Wyn Todd on rollers

8th. Had breakfast and went across to look at wall. It looks horrible (like a drainpipe) and so high. George put the bikes together and I walked round the gaff with Paula then went back to hotel. George had a go at riding and after lunch I tried it. Don't like the steep banking and the wall is terribly like a cart track, all bumps, can't seem to get more than half way up. Got fed up with the thought of it and went for a swim in the lake. Had tea and then went back to Albisgutli [sic] to get coats then wandered round, had supper and went home to bed. Exhausted with climbing stairs. Didn't sleep very well – feel unsettled.

9th. Got fixed up with crash helmets. Had another go at the wall, feel a little better, but more bumpy than ever at the top. Decided on show acts. Rudiger wants a three act. I'm not trying that, Paula says two is sufficient. Decides Hans first, myself second, George third and Hans and George double.

Have lunch. Great preparations going on all round for this big weekend. Have a walk round the town, feel unsettled still. Have tea and drive around the lake; bed early.

10th. Start at 2 p.m. Feel more settled after first show don't know how I'm going to last out 3 days of this shaking. Wall fills up very quick. Change acts around to myself first, Hans second George third then double. Feel funny with crash-hats on. Packed up for food at 7. Masses of people about – get going again at 7.30. We all stand round with our backs against the wall while he tells the nobbins tale, as if we were playing base-ball, we look like it too with our hats. Finished about 12. Very glad to have first day over. Went into wagon to check up while 'slaves' picked up the nobbins – they look good too. Very satisfied with our act, feels good to have some Swiss money in our pockets.

Sun. 11th. Wake up feeling stiff. Start again at 2 – don't know why he doesn't start earlier. Keep cracking all the afternoon – 4 shows an hour, do one or two 'ballys' between each show, even when they are coming fast. Have to stand up when we are not 'ballying' as there is only the one bike. Very good audiences, lots of cheering and shouting. It's terribly hot. Paula gives us tea in the wagon, great plates of meat and cold vegetables knock it back quick and get on with the show. The wagon girl keeps bringing round big jugs of cold coffee. Everyone seems very pleased with the business. George's mag packs up and we have to borrow a part from the bally bike. Finish again at 12. Collect nobbins again – better than Saturday.

Mon 12th. This is the big day, it starts raining at midday – it's going to ruin the business. Start about 1.30 – they roll in. Hans has got the part for George's mag. The Indian dealer comes down – funny old chap. Rains on and off all afternoon but they still come in. I have got a rotten cold, eyes and nose running all the time. We don't stop for tea. Paula sends round some sandwiches and tea. The jugs of coffee have changed to glasses of tea today and they are very welcome. We keep on packing them in and they come pretty fast this evening. Saw two of the police students that we met in Grindelwald. Pack up about 12.30, so glad to have finished for a few days and feel quite good and not too tired. Had a ride on the 'Chairs'.

Collected again had tea and bread and honey in the wagon then went to bed at 2 am.

13th. I have got flu, feel terrible, go into Zurich to get something to take. Get into a jam with a tram and scratch some paint off. Terrific excitement all round, we can't talk to anyone, so the police get into the car and we drive to the police station. We go back to our room, have a bath and I go to bed. George goes back to the station with papers to clear things up. He brings up some tea about 5.30 and I am perspiring and sneezing all the time. We take the mattress off the divan and make another bed on the floor. A gale starts blowing about 10 but it's hot and stuffy, I do not get to sleep until about 4 am.

Wed. 14th. Thank goodness we are moving out of this little room today, I feel a bit better and am glad to be moving out of Zurich, it's like London in some ways, all bustle. We go to see if we can find 'Snowy' – we find St. Nicklausen Hotel but Snowy is not here. It is such a beautiful place we are going to stay anyway and it is only 15 francs a day all in.

Thurs 15th. It's very beautiful here, the garden is a blaze of colour and slopes gently down to the lake. There is a raft for swimming, a boat house, and a small landing stage ...

The rest of the diary is about resorts they visited, not about the wall.

My mother kept accounts of how much they earned and which towns they appeared in: 10th September–13th November. Albersgutli [sic], Zurich. Herisau. St. Gallen (8 days). Basel – 18 days. Total earnings 13,123.71 Swiss Francs. I am not sure whether that is what the wall took or whether it was what my parents earned.

My mother told me they had a wonderful reception in Switzerland – often the nobbins thrown down, always money in the UK, included whole chickens, Swiss mountain sausages, Swiss cheese, rabbits and all sorts of food. However, she did not like riding the Swiss wall, which was much smaller than British ones, was not very well constructed and was fairly dangerous to ride. In between riding in various towns they spent some very nice days in the mountains, staying in nice hotels on lakesides, fishing and shopping. The diary is interesting in that it demonstrates that touring and riding a wall is not always that easy, especially in a foreign country.

Chapter 24

Wyn Todd at the 1952 Munich Oktoberfest

In my mother's recorded memories she said:

> In 1952 Kitty Muller, who owned and rode a very fine wall in Germany, asked me if I would ride for her at the Munich Oktoberfest, as she wanted to put on a show featuring Four Women of Four Nations. She had a French woman, an Italian one, herself a German, and I was to ride for England. I refused at first because I had already decided to end my riding days. However, she would not take no for an answer and in the end I went.

Kitty and Pitt wall, Munich Oktoberfest

Four international women riders, Kitty, Mia, Winnie, Odette

The Oktoberfest is a fantastic fair. Unlike England where one either has to be in the Showmen's Guild to get a position in a good fair or pay the highest price if it is a council ground, the Oktoberfest is run differently. It goes to the one who can put on the best show or ride with the best appearance. Thinking back to 1930 and the Oktoberfest where I'd worked my first big fair, I thought it would be nice to finish up there. I did wonder, it being so soon after the war, how I would go down as the English part. I was surprised at the response. Kitty and I ended the show with a double act announced as Kitty of Germany and Winnie of England – we were applauded before we started and cheered when we finished. I have great admiration for Kitty, she is a very warm-hearted person with a wonderful personality. A first-class showman and the best all-round female rider I have ever known.

Wyn Todd name badge

Wyn Todd trick riding in Munich

And so after 393 performances in the 17 days at the fair I ended my career as a Wall of Death rider.

I had enjoyed all of it; met countless good friends from all walks of life, met and married a good husband and had a lovely daughter.

My mother was 37 years old. She also kept a diary of the 17 days as follows:

16th Sep. Left Dover 12.20 arrived Ostend about 3 o'clock. Train left 5 o'clock. Had rotten compartment so found better one. Felt rotten after dinner and was sick during night, otherwise good journey.

17th Sep. Arrived Munich at 10.35, only 20 minutes late. Kitty met us and took us to the ground in her old DKW. They were just setting up the floor. She showed us our 2 x 4 sleeping compartment, then we walked round the gaff. The opposition wall was built up, and was identical, very good flash with neon, flashing signs, flags, flowers, green shrubs.

The competition was at fever pitch, each one trying to be a little better. Had lunch at 12, coffee and rolls at 4, dinner at 7 and had an early night.

18th. Very slow progress with the wall. I went into town with Kitty and had a coffee in their small cafe in the town.

19th. No signs of wall being finished, much running about and shouting. Went to Hippodrome after dinner to showmen's meeting – big noise making a long speech. Went to Hoffbrauhaus to see Kitty's husband's shooter, had some beer with the owner and danced. Enormous place like Corner House but free and easy Bavarian style.

20th. Saturday. Wall still not finished, everybody bad tempered. Thousands of people on the ground. I finally had my first try on the wall, 10 minutes before we opened. Banking like a cart track, bike good, small frame, enormous handlebars, and leads a bit on the wall. I do a double act with Kitty, hands off, wobble, a couple of clips [tricks!] then down and Kitty finished off with her trick ride. Then the 'three Act' with Kitty, Pitt and Odette. Odette has to be pushed off but rides like a demon on the wall, good act. They all ride very fast. Nobbins tale, we pick it up then Pitt takes the car on a DKW – looks twice as big as the Austin and makes a hell of a row. Kept going all day three shows an hour until 12 midnight.

21st. Start at 12 o'clock. Millions of people. 25 shows, packers. Some English showmen – saw Tommy Manning and Phil. John Collins arrived just as we closed. Has known Kitty since 1931. Had a drink in the caravan then went to Hippodrome. John came in drunk and started to get a little hanky with the showmen. We managed to get him off home without any commotion.

22nd. Monday. The English rider on the other wall calls himself Roy Swift and was supposed to bring Maureen Swift with him, looks frightened.

23rd. Tuesday. The Americans here are a tough lot don't throw any nobbins at all. Every day now much the same, open at 12 keep on ... We had a nice evening with Anin from the other wall in the cafe at the entrance to the ground, it was his birthday.

25th. Thursday. Had a late evening with Toni, Pitt, Mia and some older riders in the Hippodrome.

26th. Big ends went on my bike, rode it for three shows, then it got too bad, so closed down at 7 while they swapped the motor with the 'Bally Bike'. Could not find George to help. Gave one show again at 10, motor good.

27th. Saturday. Busy day. George took down my engine.

28th. Sunday. Biggest day so far. Spoke went on Pitt's bike, then Kitty's tyre went and later on went on the car. Kept going all day, Pitt doing repairs between shows. Anton Walbrook came along and Mia got autographs for us all. 36 shows.

30th. Tuesday. My tyre went flat and I had to have a new one on. Bike pulling up a lot.

4th October. Sunday. We were all very pleased to finish the last show without having had any spills. Pitt looked more relieved and hugged us all.

Monday. Went into town shopping, very tired. Went to dinner with Kitty and Mia at Hoffbrauhaus, then went to the P.I.

Club, nice place, good music and cheap. From there went to Heinz Club and were invited to join a party with Mr. and Mrs. Suprect, Mr. and Mrs. Heinhaus and Mrs. Schafen, and ended up at the hotel in centre of Munich, where there was a nice little band in a cage and a violinist on the dance floor. I could not drink any more champagne so drank coffee. Mr. Heinhaus asked me to sing 'Tea for Two', which they thought was wonderful. We sang several songs together and then I sang 'The Desert Song' to the accompaniment of the violin and we stayed very late, singing all the time. A very good evening.

Tuesday. Went into town again and came back to say goodbye, Kitty took us to the station and we caught the 8.15 train to Ostend. Had dinner on the train, German dinner food not too good but cheap. Had quite a good night's sleep after the carriage emptied at 1.30.

When she returned to England she wrote to *The World's Fair* about her trip, keeping the hand-written letter in her papers:

With the German Showmen by Wynne Todd.

I have just returned from Munich Fair, Germany's famous Oktoberfest, where at the request of my friend and fellow artist, Kitty Mathieu, I represented England in her International Wall of Death Show featuring 'Four Women of Four Nations', Italy, France, Germany and England.

This was my second visit to Munich, the first being in 1930, when at the aged of 15 I took part in the first Wall of Death show there. Twenty-two years had passed since that first visit and I wondered if it would have changed.

My husband and I arrived there on September 17, four days before the opening, and as we lived on the ground as guests of the Mathieu family, we were able to watch the final stages of the building up. From dawn each morning until long after dark, everyone was busy, putting their very best efforts in this, their biggest fair of the year. We watched flower boxes and shrubs being placed and hung on the rides and shows, and the track of a Dodgem being polished until it shone like a mirror. Everything was ready, gay, bright and spotless on Saturday morning, and our first performance at 11 o'clock was the beginning of twelve to fourteen hours daily of continuous performances to packed houses for 16 days.

Beer and Song. Except for the up-to-date rides and ultra-modern neon lighting, the Oktoberfest had not changed. The same masses of good natured people all in high spirits, imparting an atmosphere of gaiety to the whole impressive scene; the same enthusiastic audiences that we had in 1930; the delightful aroma of hot roast chickens and Wiener sausages that are such a great feature there; and the sound of deep-throated community singing to the brass bands coming from the wonderful buildings, erected by the breweries, each seating 5,000 people, where the beer which is brewed especially for the Oktoberfest is served only in quart mugs.

When we had closed down for the night and everything was quiet, we went into the unchanged and still popular 'Hippodrome', the restaurant built like a circus and erected only once a year for this occasion, where earlier in the evening Munich's sporting families and many famous people gather to eat, drink, and ride, or try to ride the horses around the sawdust, and where later all the showmen gather like one big family to eat an enormous supper or just to drink a grog, in the special section reserved for them, and kept open until three o'clock in the morning.

The second weekend is the peak period and by 11 o'clock on Saturday morning the ground was packed with people, many from the country villages of the Bavarian Alps, making a colourful scene in their National Costumes. Trips were run from Switzerland and France, and there were parties of visiting showmen from all parts of the world.

When the fair came to its close on Sunday night, October 5, the usual 'stripping off' began, and by noon on Monday many of the neatly covered trucks were being towed to the station where they are loaded, along with the living wagons and sometimes private cars, on to the special showman's train which takes them to their next destination. I was reminded, as I watched, of a journey we once made in Switzerland, where in our caravan, on a showman's train, we cooked and ate our evening meal while travelling through the night, at an alarming speed, from St. Gallen to Basle.

The warm-hearted welcome that many of our visiting showmen had experienced was shown to us through the whole of our stay. On our last day we dined with our hostess and a party of friends at Munich's famous Hofbrauhaus, and later we visited all the bright spots of the city's night life, where in all types of places, both Bohemian and highbrow, it is the custom to sing, as everybody does, to the accompaniment of the ever-present orchestra. We parted in the early hours of the morning, after singing together many of the much loved melodies both from their country and ours.

So ended for me a very busy but happy interlude, with more memories to add to those I already have of show people from all parts of the world. Truly 'There's no business like show business'.[1]

1. *The World's Fair*, 1 November 1952.

Chapter 25

Im Banne der Motoren Exhibition, 1995

From September 1995 to January 1996 Munich State Museum mounted a very large exhibition called '*Im Banne der Motoren, Die Steilwand-Geschichte einer Schausteller-Attraktion*' (The History of the Wall of Death, a Showground Attraction). They also published a large catalogue, which contained many photographs, advertisements, and eleven write-ups of many Wall of Death Riders (although only one was British, Maureen Swift). There was an emphasis on the German Kitty Mathieu from a Hamburg showman's family, but who had first ridden at the Oktoberfest in 1931 and, apart from the war, almost every year thereafter until she was too old to ride, and then her death in 1990.

Kitty had become, over the years, quite an icon in Munich by constantly appearing on her wall at the Oktoberfest and forever thinking up new acts, like four female riders from four nations. Also she was, apparently, one of the first, if not the first, female riders in Germany, in what was seen as a man's world of motorbikes.

There were also a lot of references and photographs relating to the Munich Oktoberfest.

What I did find surprising was that there was not a single photograph of a lion in a car on a wall.[1]

I went to see this exhibition together with my husband and the Wall of Death owner/rider Allan Ford. Even before reaching the museum this turned out to be a very emotional and traumatic experience for me. All over Munich the exhibition poster was exhibited on the underground, and in public buildings and stations. Much to my amazement the poster was an exact replica of the 1930s Oktoberfest Wall of Death poster and the exact replica of the postcard that her manager had given to my mother in 1930 signed 'To Fearless Winnie from Sam Naishtad'. It was a graphic interpretation of my mother with her riding partner Curly Lou Cody.

Im Banne Der Motoren
Exhibition poster

Alan and I had made an appointment to see one of the curators, Roland Opschondek, and we spent almost a whole day talking to him. I had taken all my 1930s photographs with me to show him. In putting the exhibition together they had contacted one or two people in the UK but not Allan or myself and as a result their information on the 1930 Oktoberfest Wall of Death – the first in Germany – was incomplete. When I told Roland about my mother he said that he had found the missing link in the first year of the wall in Munich ...

He then took us round the exhibition. So I got another surprise. The exhibition started at the *Anfang* (the beginning) and featured a 1930s photograph album belonging to a German showman's family. The page it was opened at featured the front of the wall on which my mother rode – with her standing on the bally with the other riders. The exact same photo that has been in my family since 1930. The description of the photo in the catalogue is misleading – the riders were not riding Harley Davidsons but Indians. Sam Naishtad is identified together with Crasher Evans, Speedy Bob Lee (Robert Restall), Curly Lou Cody and an 'unknown lady' – who was, of course, my mother. There is no mention in the 1930 German newspaper reports of Robert Restall riding on that wall and I believe he just happened to be standing on the bally. The rider was in fact Speedy Jo Parr, whose name, along with the other three, was written up on the bally for all to see.

Author, husband and curator in front of *Anfang* (Beginning) 1930 photo album

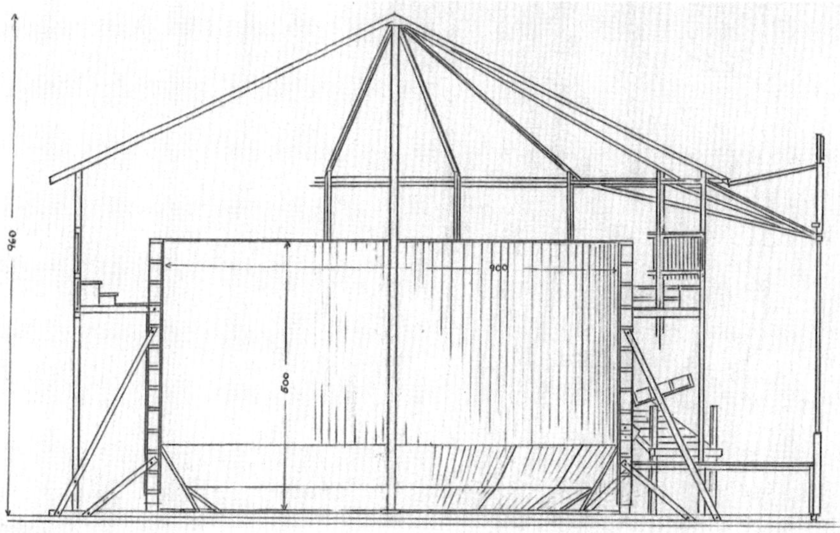

Sketch of wall building

On looking through the album there were also several other photographs, copies of which are also in my mother's album.

Author and
Amerik Steilwand Todesfahrt
1930 poster

They also showed a copy of Sam Naishtad's visiting card when he was Director of the American Silo-Drome Riders Association in London in 1929.

It was a large exhibition and even included a part of Kitty's wall, including the banking and her Indian motorbike.

Part of Kitty's wall

Kitty's Indian Scout motorbike

When I went to the museum shop and ordered ten copies of the exhibition poster they were very surprised and when I told them the lady on the poster was my mother they called the director of the museum down to meet me – and he gave me ten posters and I bought ten catalogues, for our family members.

My mother would have been so excited to have seen this exhibition and could no doubt have given the curator a lot more information than I did.

---

1. R. Opschondek, Florian Dering and Justina Schreiber, *Im Banne der Motoren.* Buchendorfer Verlag, 1995.

Chapter 26
Old Indians Never Die, They Just Have Better Stories to Tell

I hope the story of my family, their walls and their Indians has thrown more light on the history of the Wall of Death.

Recording my family history has highlighted where their Indians were taken. They have been ridden before Hitler, Mussolini, the Italian 1930s Royal Family and thc British Royal Family, both before and after the Second World War. In the 1930s before the Prince of Wales, Ramsay MacDonald the Prime Minister, Sir Henry Seagrave, Captain Malcolm Campbell, and no doubt a lot of other famous people, not to forget the locals in Abyssinia, and the public in Teheran.

They have also been ridden before thousands of the public at the 1930, 1952 and 1953 Munich Oktoberfests; the Italian public 1929–1939; the 1938 British Empire Exhibition in Glasgow; the 1939 Liege Exhibition; the Festival of Britain, 1951; the Swiss in 1949; and all over Britain from 1929 until the 1960s. Uncle Bob Todd was also responsible for introducing roller skating on the wall.

Between them they probably owned at some time between thirty and sixty Indians and eight to ten walls, three of which were actually built by Frank Todd, and numerous cars for the wall, and rode with lions and monkeys on the wall.

They have been filmed by Shell-Mex and British Pathé, interviewed for radio and shown on British TV and can now be seen on YouTube. Photographs of my family can be seen on various Wall of Death/ motorcycle websites. The Todd brothers are even on Wikipedia, although the information about which Todd brothers rode on Frank's wall at the Festival of Britain is incorrect.

In 1983 my parents, having retired from the wall, were still skiing and our local paper printed an article 'From Wall of Death to ski thrills for couple' together with the same photo of my mother at the 1952 Oktoberfest.[1]

In 1995 Allan Ford decided to employ a female rider and his efforts were filmed for TV. He appeared to have suggested that female riders were unique and revolutionary (although I don't believe Allan would suggest that since he was friendly with my late parents). After the TV show my mother's brother, Norman Soutter, wrote a letter of protest to the *Daily Mail* pointing out that his two sisters, Winifred and Gladys, 'formed the first girl Wall of Death riding team in the early thirties' and sent in a photo of my mother at the 1952 Oktoberfest.[2]

Even now my mother's career is still appearing in print. The Bugatti Owners' Club has mentioned her[3] and the Prescott Speed Hill Climb booklet had a paragraph on her 1930 appearances at New Brighton.

Photographs of my family appear all over the internet on Wall of Death and motorcycle history sites.

There is also no doubt that the wall has been a global popular culture attraction. Alan Mercer is in the process of making a list of all riders:

> I have so far forty-three different countries, 1941 recorded riders (including the pioneers I recorded that came before the perpendicular wall). 138 different riders (British and foreign) are recorded in the UK between 1929 and 1939 (39 of which were women), also twelve different wall riders were associated with having animals on the wall in that period either in cars, side-cars, three wheelers or on a motorcycle).[4]

In 2008 Dingles Fairground Heritage Centre celebrated the 80th anniversary of the Wall of Death where the Ken Fox Wall appeared. (In my opinion they got their dates wrong, they having assumed the first wall in England was in 1928 rather than 1929.) The wall is still ridden in the UK by Ken Fox, the Messhams and the Seymours.

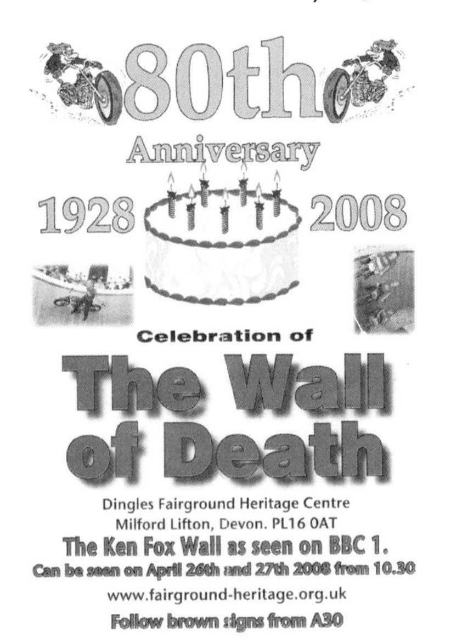

Dingles 80th anniversary flyer

Cartoons have continued to be published, my all-time favourite being the one about the lawyer.

Lawyer Cartoon

Pow cartoon

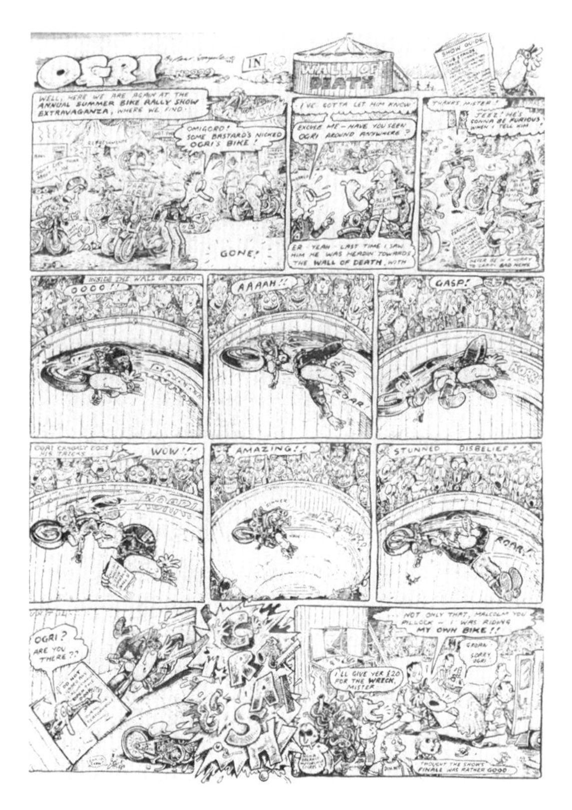

Ogri cartoon
(copyright Paul Sample)

A song was written by Richard Thompson and sung by Nanci Griffith, probably after 1973:

Let me ride on the Wall of Death one more time
Let me ride on the Wall of Death one more time
You can waste your time on the other rides
But this I the nearest to being alive
Oh let me take my chances on the Wall of Death
You can go with the crazy people in the crooked house
You can fly away on the rocket or spin in the mouse
The tunnel of love might amuse you
And Noah's Ark might confuse you
But let me take my chances on the Wall of Death
On the Wall of Death
All the world is far from me
On the Wall of Death
It's the nearest to being free
You're going nowhere when you ride on the carousel

And maybe you're strong
But what's the good of ringing a bell
The switchback will make you crazy
Beware of the bearded lady
Oh let me take my chances on the Wall of Death.

The spin-offs over the years are varied and include Wall of Death tattoos, t-shirts, embroidery kits, scale models, a Lego builder, mugs, patches, badges, greetings cards, pillows, duvet covers, tote bags, shower curtains, phone cases, leather work and even weddings in walls. Wall of Death historians are still swapping information. Several have written books, and UK walls still appear at Goodwood in Sussex, steam fairs and biker events.

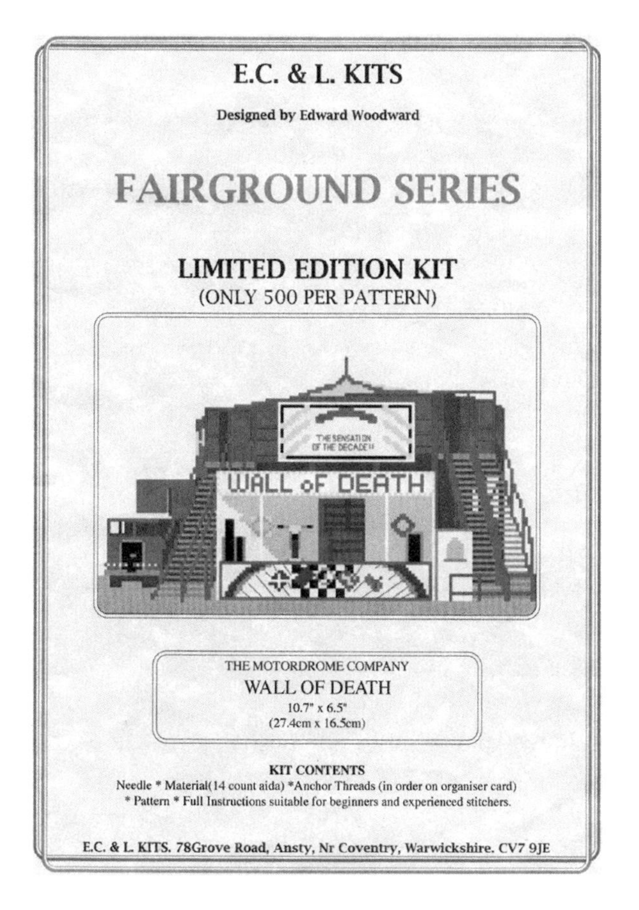

Wall of Death embroidery kit (copyright Allan Ford)

The following is a list of some of the films featuring members of my family to be seen online:

1934 British Pathé, *Taking a Lion for a Ride*, featuring Fearless Egbert, his lions and my father leading the lions into the wall.

1949 Jackie Soutter on Wyn and George Todd's wall at Clarence Pier, Southsea. Jackie is the one on the microphone. http://www.youtube.com/watch?v=oK9T72tBiFE .

Other films and TV programmes featuring the wall include:

1929 – *Kursaal, Southend.*

1941 – Film *Spare a Copper* starring George Formby – apparently Formby was so impressed with the wall he wanted to become a rider but the insurance was too expensive.

1949 – British Pathé *Wall of Death Girl* – Maureen Swift and Tornado Smith.

1951 – Film *There is Another Sun* starring Laurence Harvey (US title *Wall of Death*). The riders were the Messham family.

1956 – Film *Wall of Death*, also called *Casebook: The Case of the Wall of Death*, featuring Edgar Lustgarten, filmed at the Kursaal, Southend.

1963 – British Pathé *Wall of Death Girl* filmed at the Kursaal.

1963 – Film *Roustabout*, starring Elvis Presley.

1986 – Film *Eat the Peach* – the true story of two unemployed Irish men who built their own wall.

1995 – TV: *Girl on a Motorbike* – Allan Ford trying to find a female rider. Channel 4.

2006 – Film *The World's Fastest Indian* starring Anthony Hopkins. Tells the story of a New Zealander, Burt Munro, a life-long Indian enthusiast. In 1967 at Bonneville Salt Flats in Utah he set out to break the world speed record for the Indian and succeeded.

2012 – Documentary film *The Wall of Death* by Benedict Campbell features Ken Fox and his riders and shows details of all the work that has to be done in touring and riding.

2015 *Wall of Death Dreamland* (Margate, Kent) Part 2. See messhamswallofdeath.co.uk,

2016 TV show. Guy Martin attempted to break the record for riding a wall. He had built, using shipping containers, huge wall six metres high and 121 metres in circumference. Ken Fox taught him to ride the wall on an Indian, although Martin did not use an Indian for his televised attempt. He reached a speed of about 70 mph without blacking out or falling off. This is very interesting viewing as Martin calls in experts (not wall riders) to make sure his attempt would succeed. Available online as a DVD.

There is a motorcycle and Wall of Death museum in New York, at 250 Lake Street, Newburgh, NY 2550. They have three what they call motordromes, and a large collection of Indians, and are open on Fridays, Saturdays and Sundays. Their walls are frequently ridden for the public to see. See www.motorcyclepediamuseum.org

There is also a new museum in Sweden.

I do, however, have some unsolved mysteries which Wall of Death historians might be able to solve.

Who was Nita, who rode with Jack Todd in 1929 and possibly 1930 on Pat Collins' walls?

Who was Jill (who rode with Jack Todd as Jack and Jill), supposedly his wife (but I doubt that)?

My father was once referred to in a newspaper report as a 'famous London dirt-track rider' but I have never found evidence of that, apart from the fact that his home movies contained a lot of shots of dirt-track riding, but the riders are too far away to be identified.

Who was the boat-builder in Ramsgate, Kent, in 1932 and 1939 who built two walls for my father?

Where are the archives and photographs of Jack Todd, Bob Todd and Frank Todd junior?

Who now owns the walls which belonged to George, Jack, Bob, Frank and Frank Todd junior and Gladys Soutter?

Since 'you can't wear out an Indian Scout' who owns and rides the Indians that belonged to Jack, Bob and George Todd, Gladys and Wyn Soutter (Todd), Frank Todd Junior and Jack Lancaster?

Finally, having researched this book for over two years I have frequently stopped at 6 p.m. to watch the BBC news. Lo and behold, Ken Fox's Wall of Death has often appeared and it still does. It is one of the BBC circular Idents, which are shown between programmes.

---

1. Adsene, 5 January 1983.
2. *Daily Mail,* 6 July 1995
3. *The Autumn Classic,* 3 October 2015.
4. Alan Mercer, Wall of Death historian.

References

Personal Sources

Wyn Todd's diaries and personal letters

Photograph albums belonging to Wyn Todd, Gladys Soutter, Frank Todd and my Todd grandparents

Original press cuttings, flyers etc. kept by Wyn Todd, Gladys Soutter and Frank Todd

Recorded memories of Wyn Todd, Micky Soutter and Jackie Soutter

For Scotland, Jake Drummond, Archivist, Kirkcaldy Motor Club; and Aberdeenshire Libraries, Local Studies Senior Library Assistant, Lorraine Forbes

Bibliography

ancestry.co.uk

Andrews, Allen, *The Mad Motorists.* George G. Harrap & Co. Ltd., 1964

Braithwaite, David, *Travelling Fairs: Shire Album 17.* Shire Publications, 1976

British Empire Exhibition Official Guide, 1938 Britishnewspaperarchive.co.uk

Butlin, Sir Billy, *The Billy Butlin Story.* Robson Books, 1982

Ford, Allan and Nick Corble, *Riding the Wall of Death.* Tempus Publishing, 2006

——*You Can't Wear Out an Indian Scout.* Amberley Publishing, 2009

Drummond, Jake, *From the Archives of the Kirkcaldy and District Motor Club,* Volume 1, 2014

Gaylin, David, *The Wall of Death: Carnival Motordromes* (Images of America Series). Arcadia publishing, 2017

Manning, Ian, *700 Years of Goose Fair*. T. Bailey Forman Ltd., 1994

McNeill, Carol, *Kirkcaldy Links Market*. Fife Council Central Area Libraries

and Museums, 2004

Opschondek, R., Florian Dering and Justina Schreiber, *Im Banne der Motoren*. Buchendorfer Verlag, 1995

Rafferty, Tod, *The Indian – The History of a Classic American Motorcycle*. Bramley Books, 1998

Rennison, John RLSH, *Wings over Rutland*, 1980

South Bank Exhibition London Festival of Britain Guide, 1951

The World's Fair, 1929–1960 (reproduced by kind permission of The Worlds' Fair Ltd.)

Ware, Michael E., *Historic Fairground Scenes*. Moorland Publishing Co. Ltd., 1977

Wharton, William, *Pride (King Penguin)*. Penguin, 1987

Wilkes, Peter, *The Great Nottingham Goose Fair*. Trent Valley Publications, 1989

Woodham, Prof. J., *The Industrial Designer and the Public*. London: Pembridge History of Design Series, 1983